Adam Smith – a Primer

Adam Smith – a Primer

EAMONN BUTLER

WITH A COMMENTARY BY CRAIG SMITH

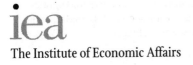

The Institute of Economic Affairs

First published in Great Britain in 2007 by
The Institute of Economic Affairs
2 Lord North Street
Westminster
London SW1P 3LB
in association with Profile Books Ltd

The mission of the Institute of Economic Affairs is to improve public understanding of the fundamental institutions of a free society, by analysing and expounding the role of markets in solving economic and social problems.

A CIP catalogue record for this book is available from the British Library.

ISBN 978 0 255 36608 3

Many IEA publications are translated into languages other than English or are reprinted. Permission to translate or to reprint should be sought from the Director General at the address above.

Typeset in Stone by MacGuru Ltd
info@macguru.org.uk

Printed and bound in Great Britain by Hobbs the Printers

CONTENTS

THE AUTHOR

Dr Eamonn Butler is Director of the Adam Smith Institute, an influential think tank that has designed policies to promote choice and competition in the delivery of essential services. He has degrees in economics, philosophy and psychology, gaining his PhD from the University of St Andrews in 1978. During the 1970s he also worked on pensions and welfare issues for the US House of Representatives in Washington, DC. On returning to the UK, he served as editor of the *British Insurance Broker* before devoting himself full time to the Adam Smith Institute, which he helped found. Dr Butler is the author of numerous books and articles on economic theory and practice, as well as the co-author of a number of books on intelligence and IQ testing.

FOREWORD

Recently appointed Professor of Commercial Economy and Mercantile Law (abbreviated later to Professor of Economic Science!) at the University of Edinburgh, I was invited to give a seminar at Harvard University in 1958, shortly after the appearance of J. K. Galbraith's *The Affluent Society*, which includes some kind words on Adam Smith. Kenneth Galbraith was much in demand in those days, and a Harvard friend believed that he had achieved a small 'coup' in arranging for me to meet him over lunch. To put his guest at his ease, he said, 'Alan, what is it like to be the holder of the most distinguished chair of economics in the world?' I was puzzled, so I recounted that the chair at Edinburgh had been originally founded and financed by the Merchant Company of Edinburgh in 1870 in the apparent belief that an economist could forecast business cycles. 'But', said KG, 'you must hold the chair that Adam Smith held.' 'Sorry,' I replied, 'wrong university, wrong subject, wrong century.' (As you all know, Adam Smith was Professor of Logic and then Moral Philosophy at Glasgow.) Our lunch was hardly a success…

I suffer a tinge of regret at having exposed KG's ignorance, because, after all, Adam Smith is closely connected with Edinburgh, even if he never held an academic appointment there. There he is buried, and, near at hand, we should soon see the first statue erected in Scotland in his honour, owing to the sterling efforts of the Adam Smith Institute and, indeed, largely to

Eamonn Butler, the writer of this splendid introduction to Smith's thinking. Moreover, like many others who have professed a knowledge, admiration and, as a Scot, almost a proprietary interest in Smith, I have tended to concentrate my attention on the text of *The Wealth of Nations*. I had failed fully to realise that, for Smith, his *The Theory of Moral Sentiments* (TMS) formed the cornerstone not only of his conception of morality but also of his analysis of views on individuals' perception of how they would, as well as should, behave in their day-to-day transactions with each other.

If for no other reason, Dr Butler's primer, buttressed by Professor Kennedy's authoritative Introduction, clearly demonstrates that there never really was an 'Adam Smith Problem' of reconciling his moral philosophy with his economic analysis. This gives the lie to the still-prevailing myth that he was a bourgeois apologist for 'capitalism' (the word does not appear anywhere in Smith) and profiteering. This explains in part one of the unusual characteristics of this text, the close attention given to an interpretation of Smith's views on the moral basis of human action in TMS, which offers justification for Dr Butler's claim that Smith should be considered primarily as a social psychologist.

I have given sufficient indication that Dr Butler has written a monograph that is not only a skilful exposition of what is known about Smith's life and times but also has an original twist in its exposition which the specialists should also savour. That completes my pleasant task, for I have no wish to hold the reader back from enjoying the work as much as I have.

ALAN PEACOCK

Honorary Professor in Public Finance,
Edinburgh Business School,
Heriot-Watt University

The views expressed in this monograph are, as in all IEA publications, those of the author and not those of the Institute (which has no corporate view), its managing trustees, Academic Advisory Council members or senior staff.

ACKNOWLEDGEMENTS

Thanks are due to Dr Madsen Pirie and Professor Gavin Kennedy for their comments on the text, and Lis Davies for her help with the quotations.

SUMMARY

- The wealth of a nation is not, as the mercantilists believed, the quantity of gold and silver in its vaults, but the total of its production and commerce – what today we would call gross domestic product.
- In a free exchange both sides become better off. Nobody would enter an exchange if they expected to lose from it. Imports are therefore just as valuable to us as exports are to others. We do not need to impoverish others to enrich ourselves. Indeed, we have more to gain if our customers are wealthy.
- Regulations on commerce are ill founded and counterproductive. Prosperity is threatened by taxes, import tariffs, export subsidies and preferences for domestic industries.
- A nation's productive capacity rests on the division of labour and the accumulation of capital it makes possible. Huge increases in output can be gained by breaking down production into many small tasks, each undertaken by specialist hands. This leaves producers with a surplus for investment.
- A country's future income depends on the rate of capital accumulation. The more that is invested in better productive processes, the more wealth will be created in the future.

- When there is free trade and competition the market system automatically remains focused on the most urgent needs. Where things are scarce, people are prepared to pay more for them. There is more profit in supplying them, so producers invest capital in order to produce more.
- Prosperity grows most rapidly when there is an open, competitive marketplace, with free exchange and without coercion. Defence, justice and the rule of law are needed to maintain this openness. Freedom and self-interest do not lead to chaos, but – as if guided by an 'invisible hand' – produce order and concord.
- Vested interests use government power to distort the market system for their own benefit. Employers and professionals may promote regulations that stifle competition, such as entry barriers that prevent people from practising particular trades.
- Taxes should be proportionate to income and ought to be certain and convenient to pay. They should be cheap to collect, should not hamper business, should not be so onerous as to encourage evasion and should not require frequent visits from tax gatherers.
- Human beings have a natural 'sympathy' (or empathy) for others. This enables them to moderate their behaviour and preserve harmony. It is also the basis of moral judgements about behaviour and the source of human virtue. Human nature is a better guide to the creation of a harmonious society than the overweening reason of zealots and visionaries.

INTRODUCTION
Gavin Kennedy[1]

Eamonn Butler has written an admirable and authoritative introduction to Adam Smith, the man and his thinking. This is the best short introduction to him in print that I know of, and it will enable anybody to know what Smith was truly about.

Eamonn Butler steers well clear of controversies about Adam Smith's political economy, of which much has been written over the years. The account of Smith, the person and his books is an accurate assessment of his unique synthesis of the evolution of British society up to the second half of the eighteenth century.

Adam Smith published his lesser-known book, *The Theory of Moral Sentiments*, seventeen years before *An Inquiry into the Nature and Causes of the Wealth of Nations*. From the gap between them it is asserted that Smith replaced the moral value of benevolence with amoral self-interest as the motivator of human action. From notes scribed by anonymous students in 1762–3, we know that large portions of Smith's lectures reappeared almost verbatim in *The Wealth of Nations* in 1776. He published his lectures (1751–64) on ethics as *The Theory of Moral Sentiments* (1759). So Adam Smith did not hold contradictory views about human motivation.

Smith was a moral philosopher. Economics in the eighteenth century was not yet the separate discipline it became in the late

1   Gavin Kennedy is Professor Emeritus at Heriot-Watt University and author of *Adam Smith's Lost Legacy*, published by Palgrave Macmillan in 2005.

nineteenth century. True, there were many earlier and contemporary authors of pamphlets on economic subjects (Yale University holds several thousand from the sixteenth to the eighteenth centuries), and some of their authors made contributions to economics, but none produced a comprehensive inquiry on the scale and of the kind attempted by Adam Smith.

Before Smith, political economy focused on the enrichment of the sovereign and the state with gold and silver bullion to finance foreign wars. *The Wealth of Nations* refocused political economy on to the enrichment of consumers from the 'annual product of land and labour'. It was not a textbook; it specifically discusses the nature of wealth and what causes it to grow.

Books I and II set out the distinctive features of human society, such as the propensity to exchange, divisions of labour, factors of production, dynamics of markets, and the distribution of revenue among the participants. Book III places eighteenth-century Britain in the context of the social evolution of society, from primitive 'hunting', through 'shepherding' and 'agriculture', to the age of commerce, and shows how the fall of Rome in the fifth century interrupted this 'natural' progression in western Europe.

When Europe began to recover after the fifteenth century, it did so under the burdens of policies serving what Smith called 'mercantile commerce', which Book IV criticises sharply for its primary error that the nation's wealth consisted of the accumulation of gold and silver bullion, and that the trade balance mattered because a country must export more than it imports. Worse, it believed that the domestic economy was stronger from having protective monopolies, restrictions on the hiring and mobility of labour, and from interferences with natural market freedoms.

Smith's remedies for these errors centred on freeing markets from interventions that altered their natural working. He favoured extending the free exchange of competitively produced output to allow the natural rate of economic growth to commence by enabling people to combine 'land, labour or capital' with others, to produce goods for sale in markets. After paying rents to landlords, wages to labourers and profits to merchants and manufacturers, owners of capital would reinvest their net profits in additional productive activities and, through successive rounds of production and exchange, create real wealth from the annual produce of the land and labour of the society, which would continue to grow slowly and gradually through successive cycles of the 'great wheel of circulation'.

In Book V, Smith addressed the appropriate roles of governments, setting out their basic functions: defence; justice; public works and institutions that facilitated commerce; the education of 'people of all ages'; measures against 'loathsome and offensive diseases'; the maintenance of the 'dignity of the sovereign'; and the financing of these expenditures through taxation and charges to the beneficiaries (in preference to public debt).

The Wealth of Nations addressed the uniquely damaging mercantile 'principles of political œconomy' of his age, as they had evolved in the recovery of Europe from the fall of Rome and the millennium-long emergence of nation-states from warlords and feudalism. The past two hundred years provide many examples of authors judging Smith's books with the advantages of two centuries of additional work and research, to which they stand up remarkably well.

The majority of the people in western Europe were desperately poor and their absolute poverty and persecution were the main drivers of emigration to North America, South Africa and

Australasia, through to the early decades of the twentieth century. Smith saw beyond the facts of poverty to its cause, namely the absence of wealth creation. Relief comes only from within societies, by their creation of the conditions that create wealth. It was to this problem that he directed his historical approach to the study of humankind. Smith's texts are sprinkled throughout with examples and quotations from the classical Greek and Latin texts in which he was thoroughly versed. Like all the major figures of the eighteenth-century Enlightenment, he looked backwards to the origins of society and not forwards to versions of utopia; such romanticism thrived in the nineteenth, not the eighteenth, century.

Europe's civilisation slumped into warlord barbarism and feudalism, but also, slowly and gradually (a phrase common throughout his work), agricultural output recovered, the population grew and commerce restarted in scattered fairs and markets. In the hundred years before 1760 the range of domestic articles, even in the poorest homes of common labourers, showed a degree of comparative 'opulence' (much of it due to second-hand acquisitions) superior to that of the North American hunting tribes and their most powerful 'princes'. From the reports of travellers, combined with his observations of nearby small nail and pin factories and forges around Kirkcaldy, Smith saw the creation of real wealth not in the form of gold and silver bullion, but in the production and distribution of the albeit crude output of the land and labour of society then becoming visible in the homes of the working population, which was a real barometer of a country's relative opulence.

His initial insight was not in discovering the division of labour – that 'honour' went back to Plato and, in 'modern' times, to

Sir William Petty (1690) – but in realising its significance as the means by which real opulence could spread among the majority of the population and not just to the very richest of them, and make them all progressively more opulent within a few generations.

That led him to ask: if the division of labour is the key, what conditions would increase output; how would each person's share be determined; and, crucially, what obstacles stood in the way of this happening? In his leap from description to analysis he took the first step towards the foundations of the new science of economics.

I offer the following brief summary of his model of a commercial economy operating in perfect liberty, which is complementary to Eamonn Butler's excellent presentation, which follows.

Commercial society develops exchanges of the marketable products of the division of labour. Barter, the direct but inefficient exchange of goods for goods, long preceded the appearance of the more efficient indirect exchange using money. The existence of coinage in ancient civilisations several millennia ago shows the early existence of commerce from the division of labour (why else would they need coinage?).

The earliest exchanges were between the products of the countryside (food and raw materials) and those of small towns (primitive manufactured tools and trinkets). Market prices of goods in exchange are decided by supply and effectual demand, and may differ from what Smith called 'natural prices', in which the rewards to the owners of the factors of production (land, labour and capital), cooperating in production, exactly match their costs, including the local natural rate of profit. Market prices, forever oscillating around, but never settling at, a perfect equilibrium, may not earn their costs. Changing market prices, however, signal participants to pay more or less for, and to supply more or less of, available products, with actual supply necessarily adjusting to these signals over time. These constitute the dynamics of a competitive economy.

Labour is either productive or unproductive, the distinction dependent upon whether labour, in combination with fixed capital, produces goods that are sold in markets and earn their costs, including the profits of enterprise. Those products of unproductive labour (for example, menial servants serving a rich family's dinner) that do not sell in markets to earn their costs are consumption out of revenue; the products of productive labour, however, earn their costs and reproduce net revenue (profit), which may be used for consumption (prodigality) or for net investment (frugality). Nations grow wealthier from having in them a higher proportion of frugal producers compared with the proportion of prodigal consumers over a time period. From its annual rate of net investment, an economy increases employment (raising the wages of labour and spreading opulence among the least well-off majority), which increases the annual output of the 'necessaries, conveniences and amusements of life'.

Unfortunately, the fall of Rome interrupted this natural process and by the time the economy recovered a millennium later and took advantage of the improvements in farming technologies, and the new technological potential from the renaissance in the sciences, societies had developed political institutions, including religious dogmatisms, that legislated for false mercantile ideas which acted to inhibit the natural evolution of the economy.

Perfect liberty was compromised with statutes enforcing tariffs, duties and prohibitions against free trade and from town guilds and craft monopolies that reduced the benefits of competitive free entry and exit from markets. They also prohibited the natural right of labour to work in trades in which they had not served long apprenticeships, prevented individuals from selling or buying products not produced in specific localities and, in pursuit of the mercantile mirage of the trade balance, imposed duties, drawbacks and bounties on imports and exports to the detriment of consumers.

The worrying fact is that many of the inhibitions on maintaining a positive rate of net investment that concerned Adam Smith remain with us in the 21st century, similarly promoted by mercantile-minded legislatures and populist falsehoods. Today, in the global economy, with absolute poverty in the developed countries no longer the problem it was in Smith's day, the problem of absolute and relative poverty in the developing and non-developing countries in the world should move the hearts of all economists, as it did the heart and mind of Adam Smith, who in retrospect was the first economist.

Almost all the so-called diversions and detailed expositions supposedly causing *The Wealth of Nations* to be 'difficult' and 'irrelevant' to modern readers arise from misunderstandings of what he was about. He was not a modern-style author of a 'principles of economics' text – the subject did not exist when Smith was alive. He wrote a report of his inquiry into the true meaning of national wealth, what caused wealth to grow and society to progress towards opulence, and what held it back. His was the right book at the right time. That was his genius and his legacy. And Eamonn Butler's presentation is your best opportunity to see why.

Adam Smith – a Primer

1   WHY ADAM SMITH IS IMPORTANT

Adam Smith (1723–90) was a Scottish philosopher and econo-mist who is best known as the author of *An Inquiry into the Nature and Causes of the Wealth of Nations* (1776), one of the most influ-ential books ever written. Smith transformed our thinking about the principles of economic life, from an ancient to a distinctively modern form, based on a completely new understanding of how human society works.

The old view of economics

So much did Smith change our ideas, indeed, that it is hard even to describe the economic system that prevailed in his time. Called *mercantilism*, it measured national wealth in terms of a country's stock of gold and silver. Importing goods from abroad was seen as damaging because it meant that this supposed wealth must be given up to pay for them; exporting goods was seen as good because these precious metals came back. Trade benefited only the seller, not the buyer; and one nation could get richer only if others got poorer.

On the basis of this view, a vast edifice of controls was erected in order to prevent the nation's wealth draining away – taxes on imports, subsidies to exporters and protection for domestic industries. Even Britain's own American colonies were penalised under this system, with disastrous results. Indeed, all commerce was looked upon with suspicion and the culture of protectionism pervaded the domestic economy too. Cities prevented artisans from other towns moving in to ply their trade; manufacturers and merchants petitioned the king for protective monopolies; labour-saving devices such as the new stocking-frame were banned as a threat to existing producers.

The productivity of free exchange

Smith showed that this vast mercantilist edifice was based on a mistake, and was counterproductive. He argued that in a free exchange both sides became better off. Quite simply, nobody would enter an exchange if they expected to lose from it. The buyer profits, just as the seller does. Imports are just as valuable to us as our exports are to others. We do not need to impoverish others to enrich ourselves: indeed, we have more to gain if our customers are wealthy.[1]

Given the essential truth that free exchange benefits both sides, Smith maintained that trade and exchange increase our prosperity just as surely as do agriculture or manufacture. The wealth of a nation is not the quantity of gold and silver in its vaults, but the total of its production and commerce – what today we would call gross domestic product.

It was a novel idea, but a very powerful one. It blew a large intellectual hole through the trade walls that had been erected around European states since the sixteenth century. And it had practical

---

1   *The Wealth of Nations*, Book IV, ch. III, part II, p. 493, para. c9. (Page numbers in the notes refer to *The Glasgow Edition of the Works and Correspondence of Adam Smith*. See Select Bibliography.)

results too. *The Wealth of Nations*, with its direct, pungent, challenging style, sardonic wit and a multitude of examples, was accessible to practical people, who would translate its ideas into action.

The book came too late to head off war with the American colonies, but it laid the groundwork for Prime Minister William Pitt's advocacy of free trade and tax simplification, and Sir Robert Peel's later measures to liberalise the agricultural markets. Arguably, then, it was the foundation of the great nineteenth-century era of free trade and economic expansion. Even today the common sense of free trade is accepted throughout the world, whatever the practical difficulties of achieving it.

Social order based on freedom

Smith could not anticipate such influence. But this growing confidence in personal and commercial freedom stemmed directly from his radical, fresh understanding of how human societies actually worked. He realised that social harmony would emerge naturally as human beings struggled to find ways to live and work with each other. Freedom and self-interest need not lead to chaos, but – as if guided by an 'invisible hand' – would produce order and concord.

They would also bring about the most efficient possible use of resources. As free people struck bargains with others – solely in order to better their own condition – the nation's land, capital, skills, knowledge, time, enterprise and inventiveness would be drawn automatically and inevitably to the ends and purposes that people valued most highly.

Thus the maintenance of a prospering social order did not require the continued supervision of kings and ministers. It would grow organically as a product of human nature. To grow best and to work most efficiently, however, it required an open, competitive marketplace, with free exchange and without coercion. It needed rules to maintain this openness, just as a fire-basket is needed to contain a fire. But those rules, the rules of justice and morality, are general and impersonal, quite unlike the specific and personal interventions of the mercantilist authorities.

The Wealth of Nations was therefore not just a study of *economics* as we understand it today, but a groundbreaking treatise on human social psychology: about life, welfare, political institutions, the law and morality.

The psychology of ethics

Smith came from a time when it was possible for an educated intellectual to know everything – about science, the arts, literature, philosophy, classics and ethics. And he did. He amassed a huge library and planned a history of the liberal arts, as well as a book on law and government. And it was not *The Wealth of Nations* that first made his reputation, but a book on ethics, *The Theory of Moral Sentiments*. It is less well known today, but at the time it was just as influential as *The Wealth of Nations* and just as important to its author.

The Theory of Moral Sentiments attempts to identify the basis on which we form moral judgements. Once again, Smith sees it as a matter of deep human psychology. Human beings have a natural 'sympathy' (today we would say 'empathy') for others that enables them to understand how to moderate their behaviour and preserve harmony. It is the basis of moral judgements about behaviour, and the source of human virtue.

Self-interest and virtue

Some people today wonder how the self-interest that drives Smith's economic system can be reconciled with the 'sympathy' that drives his ethics. Here is his answer: 'How selfish soever man may be supposed, there are evidently some principles in his nature, which interest him in the fortune of others, and render their happiness necessary to him, though he derives nothing from it except the pleasure of seeing it.'[2]

In other words, human nature is complex. The baker does not supply us with bread out of benevolence; but nor is it self-interest which prompts someone to dive into a river to save a drowning stranger. Smith's books are complementary attempts to identify how self-interested human beings can – and do – live together peacefully (in the moral sphere) and productively (in the economic).

But then *The Wealth of Nations* is certainly no endorsement of dog-eat-dog capitalism, as it is sometimes caricatured. Self-interest may drive the economy, but if there is genuinely open competition and no coercion, that is a force for good. And in any event, Smith's own humanity and benevolence colour every page. He lifts the welfare of the nation, and of the poor in particular, above the special interests of the merchants and the mighty, chastising the manufacturers who try to thwart free competition and condemning the governments who help them.

Human nature and human society

Eighteenth-century thinkers came to believe that there must be a

---

2   *The Theory of Moral Sentiments*, part I, ch. I, p. 9, para. 1.

sounder foundation for society than the dogma handed down by the clerics or the imperatives issued by the political authorities. Some struggled to find 'rational' systems of law and ethics. But Smith argued that human society – including science, language, the arts and commerce – was rooted deeply in human nature. He showed how our natural instincts are a better guide than any over-vaunting reason. If we simply remove 'all systems either of preference or of restraint'[3] and rely on 'natural liberty', we will find ourselves settling, unintentionally but surely, into a harmonious, peaceful and efficient social order.

This liberal social order does not require the constant attention of kings and ministers to conserve it. But it does rely on human beings observing certain rules of interpersonal conduct – such as justice and respect for other people's lives and property. The beneficial overall social order then emerges quite naturally. Smith's quest was to identify the natural principles of human behaviour that in fact create this fortunate result.

---

3   *The Wealth of Nations*, Book IV, ch. IX, part II, p. 687, para. 51.

2 SMITH'S LIFE AND CAREER

Margaret Douglas was already pregnant when her husband, a well-connected lawyer and former customs officer, died in January 1723. On 5 June she registered the birth of their child, to whom she gave her late husband's name: Adam Smith. The boy would mature to become one of the leading thinkers of his age and author of one of the most influential books ever written.

Kirkcaldy and Glasgow

We know little of his early years, except that at the age of three he was briefly abducted by gypsies, until recovered by his uncle. But the everyday life of his birthplace must have provided him with much of the material that would inform his later career. The Scottish port of Kirkcaldy, across the Firth of Forth from Edinburgh, was a trading centre, with ships landing fish, exporting coal from the local mines and bringing back scrap iron for the iron-working industry.[1] Smith grew up alongside the sailors, fish merchants, nail-makers, customs officers and smugglers whose trades he would describe in *The Wealth of Nations*.

Yet things were changing; growing trade with the Americas, in commodities like tobacco and cotton, favoured modern

---

1   E. G. West, *Adam Smith: The Man and His Works*, Liberty Fund, Indianapolis, IN, 1976, p. 31.

western ports like Glasgow over antiquated eastern harbours like Kirkcaldy.[2] Smith's great book would also record such shifting patterns of trade and of the lives of the communities who depended on it.

At school, his passion for books and his extraordinary memory became apparent. He went on to Glasgow University at the age of fourteen (quite a normal age at the time), where he studied under the great moral philosopher Francis Hutcheson – libertarian, rationalist, utilitarian, plain speaker and thorn in the side of authority – who seems to have infected Smith with some of the same characteristics.

Oxford and incentives

Smith excelled, and won a scholarship to Balliol College, Oxford. In 1740, now just seventeen, he saddled up for the month-long horseback journey. If thriving, commercial Glasgow had been an eye-opener to a boy from backward Kirkcaldy, England seemed a different world. He wrote of the grandness of its architecture and the fatness of its cattle, quite unlike the poor specimens of his native Scotland.

But the English education system did not impress him. Indeed, it gave him an important lesson on the power of perverse incentives, which he would catalogue acidly in *The Wealth of Nations*. Oxford teachers were paid from large college endowments, not from students' fees. As a result, in Oxford 'the greater part of the public professors have, for these many years,

---

2   R. H. Campbell and A. S. Skinner, *Adam Smith*, Croome Helm, London, 1982, pp. 9–10.

given up altogether even the pretence of teaching',[3] and college life was contrived 'for the interest, or more properly speaking, for the ease of the masters'.[4] Smith's economic education was continuing apace.

Thanks to Balliol's world-class library, however, Smith was able to educate himself in the classics, literature and other subjects. He left Oxford in 1746, before the expiry of his scholarship, to return to Kirkcaldy, where he spent two years writing on literature, physics, logic and scientific method.

Early lecturing career

Through family contacts, Lord Kames, a leading lawyer and thinker, invited him to give a series of public lectures in Edinburgh on English literature and on the philosophy of law. From these lectures, we can see that even in his twenties Smith was already working out many of the key ideas (such as the division of labour) that would form the essential foundations of *The Wealth of Nations* much later.

The lectures were a great success and the stepping stone to his next career move. In 1751, aged 27, he went back to the University of Glasgow, this time to teach logic, moral philosophy, literature and rhetoric. (At the time, 'rhetoric' had none of today's implications and meant only the study of style and communication.)

His philosophy course covered theology, ethics, jurisprudence and public policy. The lectures on jurisprudence and policy (surviving only in students' notes) contain many of the ideas (such

---

3 *The Wealth of Nations*, Book V, ch. I, part III, article II, p. 761, para. f8.
4 Ibid., Book V, ch. I, part III, article II, p. 764, para. f15.

as the workings of the price system, the shortcomings of protectionism and the development of governmental and economic institutions) that would appear almost verbatim in *The Wealth of Nations* years later.

But it was Smith's reflections on ethics that would make his fortune. In 1759 he published them as *The Theory of Moral Sentiments*. Stylish and original, it explained our moral judgements in terms of human social psychology. Smith's friend, the philosopher and historian David Hume, sent copies to a number of his friends – and one, the statesman Charles Townshend, was so impressed that he promptly hired Smith, at a generous salary of £300 payable for life, as personal tutor to his stepson, the young Duke of Buccleuch.

Travels

Though intellectually brilliant, Smith was an odd choice for a personal tutor. The writer James Boswell said that he had 'a mind crowded with all manner of subjects', making him notoriously absent-minded. Once, lost in thought, he brewed bread and butter instead of tea; another time, mulling over some problem, he walked the eight miles to Dunfermline, before realising where he was; and he fell into a ditch because he was not concentrating on the road ahead.

But before long, Smith and his pupil set off for France. Travel was part of the education of every young aristocrat of that time. In Paris they enjoyed the sparkling company of David Hume, who was private secretary to the ambassador there. But Smith's spoken French was very poor and he found it hard to make other contacts. Boredom set in and he told Hume, 'I have begun to write a book to pass away the time.'[5] The book was *The Wealth of Nations*.

In his subsequent journeys, through the South of France, to Geneva, and back to Paris, Smith picked up fact upon fact about the culture, government, commerce, regulation and economic life of Europe, and reflected on the differences to those at home. Discussions with some of the Continent's leading luminaries further sharpened the thinking he was doing on his great book.

The Wealth of Nations

The pair returned to London in 1766. Smith settled back in Kirkcaldy, where he could now afford a substantial High Street house, which he shared with his mother and cousin Janet. (Smith remained devoted to his mother until her death in 1784. He never married, though apparently he had one early attachment 'to a young lady of great beauty and accomplishment'.[6])

He spent many years in Kirkcaldy, writing, revising and polishing his manuscript – at some cost to his health. But he was revived by a long period in London from 1773 to 1776, during which he enjoyed the company of other great minds, including the painter Sir Joshua Reynolds, the ancient historian Edward Gibbon, the radical politician Edmund Burke, Boswell and even (despite their conflicting views) the lexicographer Dr Samuel Johnson.

At last, *The Wealth of Nations* was published in March 1776. It was a great commercial success, appearing in many editions and many languages within just a few years. It was a practical success

---

5   Letter to David Hume dated 5 July 1764.
6   D. Stewart, 'Account of the life and writings of Adam Smith LLD', 1794, in *The Glasgow Edition*, vol. III, note K, pp. 349–50.

too: its prescriptions, such as trade liberalisation, started making their way into public policy.

Commissioner of Customs

Smith was rewarded with the post of Commissioner of Customs in Edinburgh, on a handsome salary of £600. The arch-critic of Britain's arbitrary and inefficient customs system was now in a position to do something about it, and he was diligent in this work.[7] He advised on other issues too – against trade restrictions on Ireland, for example, and on the American colonial 'disturbances'. Later, Prime Minister William Pitt adopted Smith's principles in forging a trading pact with France and in implementing a widespread reform of the nation's tax system.

Smith loved discussion and debate with friends. In July 1790, during one of many such evenings in Edinburgh, he felt tired and retired to bed, saying that the discussion would need to continue in some other place. He died a few days later and was buried under a generous but restrained monument in the churchyard near his Canongate home.

7   Campbell and Skinner, *Adam Smith*, pp. 200–203.

3   *THE WEALTH OF NATIONS*

The book's broad themes

Adam Smith wrote *The Wealth of Nations* partly to provoke politicians out of their policy of restricting and distorting commerce, rather than letting it flourish. So he uses plain language, which is still accessible today.

But Smith was also trying to create a new science of economics. It was pioneering work, and his terms and concepts can be hard to reconcile with today's. His text is discursive, full of long digressions and afforested with facts, from the price of silver in China to the diet of Irish prostitutes in London. All this makes his book hard to navigate. So let us first focus on some of its main themes.

The most obvious theme is that *regulations on commerce are ill-founded and counterproductive*. The prevailing view at the time was the 'mercantilist' idea that a nation's wealth was the amount of money that it possessed. This implied that to become richer, a nation needed to sell as much as possible to others, in order to get as much coin as possible in return; and it needed to buy as little as possible from others, in order to prevent its cash reserves leaking abroad. This view of trade led to the creation of a vast network of import tariffs, export subsidies, taxes and preferences for domestic industries, all designed to limit imports and promote exports.

Smith's revolutionary view was that wealth is not about how

much gold and silver sits in a nation's vaults. *The real measure of a nation's wealth is the stream of goods and services that it creates.* He had invented the idea, so common and fundamental in economics today, of gross domestic product.[1] And the way to maximise that product, he argued, was not to restrict the nation's productive capacity, but to set it free.

Another central theme is that this *productive capacity rests on the division of labour* and the *accumulation of capital* that makes it possible. Huge efficiencies can be won by breaking production down into many small tasks, each undertaken by specialist hands. This leaves producers with a surplus that they can exchange with others, or use to invest in new and even more efficient labour-saving machinery.

Smith's third theme is that a country's *future income depends upon this capital accumulation*. The more that is invested in better productive processes, the more wealth will be created in the future. But if people are going to build up their capital, they must be confident that it will be secure from theft. The countries that prosper are those that grow their capital, manage it well and protect it.

A fourth theme is that *this system is automatic*. Where things are scarce, people are prepared to pay more for them: there is more profit in supplying them, so producers invest more capital in order to produce more. Where there is a glut, prices and profits are low and producers switch their capital and enterprise elsewhere. Industry thus remains focused on the nation's most important needs, without the need for central direction.

But *the system is automatic only when there is free trade and*

---

1   A point made neatly by P. J. O'Rourke, *On The Wealth of Nations*, Atlantic Monthly Press, New York, 2006, pp. 7–8.

competition. When governments grant subsidies or monopolies to favoured producers, or shelter them behind tariff walls, they can charge higher prices. The poor suffer most from this, facing higher costs for the necessities that they rely on.

A further theme of *The Wealth of Nations* is how *different stages of economic progress produce different government institutions*. The early hunter-gatherers had little of any value. But when people became farmers, their land, crops and livestock were important property and they developed government and justice systems to protect it.

In the age of commerce, as people accumulate capital, property becomes even more significant. But this age is populated by merchants who have much to gain from distorting markets in their favour and who have the guile to use the political process to help them. *Competition and free exchange are under threat from the monopolies, tax preferences, controls and other privileges that producers are able to extract from the government authorities.*

For all these reasons, Smith believes that *government must be limited*. It has core functions such as maintaining defence, keeping order, building infrastructure and promoting education. It should keep the market economy open and free, and not act in ways that distort it.

Production and exchange

The first of the five 'Books' in *The Wealth of Nations* explains the mechanisms of production and exchange, and their contribution to national income.

The benefits of specialisation

Using the example of a pin factory, Smith shows that the *division of labour* – labour specialisation – generates enormous increases in output. Pin-making seems a 'trifling manufacture', but is really quite complicated. Wire must be drawn out, straightened, cut and pointed. The top must be ground flat for the head, which in turn must be made and affixed. The pins must be whitened and put into paper. Indeed, there are about eighteen different operations in the process.

A single person, he says, doing all these different operations, could probably not make as many as twenty pins in a day (and if they also had to mine and smelt the metal required, perhaps not even one pin a year). But in the factory the work is divided between different people, each of whom does only one or two of the separate operations. Between them, the ten-strong team of pin-makers can actually make 48,000 pins in a day – equivalent to 4,800 each, or 240 times the daily output achievable by a single person.

This specialisation is so efficient that it emerges not just within companies, but between industries and even between countries. Farmers specialise in raising crops or livestock: their land is consequently much better tended, and more productive, than if they had to spend time making all their household items too. But manufacturers are very happy to supply household goods and leave the production of their food to the farmers. Similarly, countries specialise by exporting the goods they produce best and importing the goods that others produce better.

The increased efficiency comes not just from the skill acquired when people do the same task many times, says Smith. Less time is wasted in moving from one operation to another, and specialisation allows people to use dedicated, labour-saving machinery to increase output even further. Consequently: 'The greatest improvement in the productive powers of labour, and the greater part of the skill, dexterity, and judgement with which it is any where directed, or applied, seem to have been the effects of the division of labour.'[2]

The division of labour harnesses the cooperation of many thousands of people in the production of even the most basic of everyday objects:

> The woollen coat, for example, which covers the day-
> labourer, as coarse and rough as it may appear, is the
> produce of the joint labour of a great multitude of workmen.
> The shepherd, the sorter of the wool, the wool-comber or
> carder, the dyer, the scribbler, the spinner, the weaver,
> the fuller, the dresser, with many others, must all join
> their different arts in order to complete even this homely
> production.[3]

Moreover, the transportation of the wool will have required sailors, shipwrights and sail-makers; even the shears for cutting the wool would need miners and ironworkers. The list seems endless. But this collaboration of thousands of highly efficient specialists is the source of developed countries' great wealth, and makes items such as woollen coats accessible even to the poorest – what Smith calls 'that universal opulence which extends itself to the lowest ranks of the people'.[4]

---

2   *Wealth of Nations*, Book I, ch. I, p. 13, para. 1.
3   Ibid., Book I, ch. I, p. 22, para. 11.
4   Ibid., Book I, ch. I, p. 22, para. 10.

The mutual gains from exchange

Smith's quintessential Chapter II explains how *material exchange* spreads the benefits of this productive efficiency around the community. Through some particular mental or physical talents, he conjectures, one person in a 'primitive country' might be better than others at making arrows, while another is better at metal-working. By specialising, the fletcher produces more arrows, and the smith more blades, than either can use. So they exchange arrows for blades. Both now have a useful mix of tools and each has benefited from the other's efficient, specialised production.

The propensity to 'truck, barter, and exchange', claims Smith, is a natural and universal feature of human behaviour, precisely because both parties benefit. Indeed, the exchange would not occur if either side thought themselves the loser by it. And this is a crucial insight. In Smith's world, like ours, most goods were exchanged for money rather than bartered for other goods. Since money was regarded as wealth, it seemed that only the seller could benefit from the process. But Smith shows that the benefit is mutual. By exchanging, both sides get the goods they want for less effort than they would have to expend in making them for themselves. Each is made richer by the exchange. Wealth, in other words, is not fixed, but is *created* by human commerce. It was a groundbreaking idea.

Another crucial insight is that exchange still benefits both sides, even though each party proposes and accepts the bargain entirely in their own self-interest and not with the other side's welfare in mind. That is fortunate, because it gives us a way to induce other people to part with things we want. In Smith's famous words:

> It is not from the benevolence of the butcher, the brewer, or
> the baker, that we expect our dinner, but from their regard
> to their own interest. We address ourselves, not to their
> humanity but to their self-love, and never talk to them of
> our own necessities but of their advantages.[5]

By 'self-love' or 'self-interest', Smith does not imply 'greed' or 'selfishness'. His meaning is an eighteenth-century one: not some unpleasant readiness to gain by making others worse off, but an entirely due and appropriate concern to look after our own welfare. This is so natural and important to human beings that in *The Theory of Moral Sentiments* he calls it 'prudence'.[6] In the same book, he stresses that 'sympathy' (or as we would say, empathy) for others is one of humanity's salient characteristics, and justice (not doing harm to others) is one of its fundamental rules.

Wider markets bring bigger gains

The benefits we get from exchange are what drive us to specialise and so increase the surplus that we can exchange with others. Just how far that specialisation can go depends on the extent to which exchange is possible, says Smith – that is, on the extent of the *market*.[7] Only a 'great town' provides enough customers for porters, for example; while scattered communities may be unable to support even specialist carpenters or stonemasons, forcing people to do more of these tasks for themselves.

One thing that definitely does extend the market is *money*.[8]

---

5   Ibid., Book I, ch. II, pp. 26–7, para. 12.

6   *The Theory of Moral Sentiments*, part VI, section I.

7   *The Wealth of Nations*, Book I, ch. III.

8   Ibid., Book I, ch. IV.

Life would be tedious if hungry brewers always had to search out thirsty bakers. That is why we commonly use the medium of money – exchanging our surplus product for money, then exchanging money back for other products that we want.

The index of value

But, whether mediated through money or not, what is it that determines the rate at which different products are exchanged? It was a puzzle to Smith that something essentially useless (like a diamond) has a high 'value in exchange', when something vital (like water) has almost none. Today we might solve it with marginal utility theory: since diamonds are so rare, an additional one is a great prize; but since water is so plentiful, an extra cupful is actually of little use to us. Or we might invoke supply and demand analysis.

Unfortunately, the first tool did not yet exist and, at this point in *The Wealth of Nations*, Smith had not yet perfected the second. So he struggles to identify what it is about a product which gives it a particular value.

It seemed natural to him that in primitive societies, value originally must have reflected the *labour* put into the item's production.[9] After all, we put 'toil and trouble' into creating the product we sell precisely to spare ourselves the effort of creating the product we buy. There is no point in either side buying something they could create with less effort themselves; so the ideal rate of exchange should reflect equal effort.

Therefore if among hunters 'it usually costs twice the labour

---

9   Ibid., Book I, ch. V.

to kill a beaver which it does to kill a deer, one beaver should naturally exchange for or be worth two deer'.[10] Of course, Smith observes, not all labour is equal. One production process may be harder work, or require more ingenuity, or demand a long period of training and experience. But these factors will be accounted for 'by the higgling and bargaining in the market'.[11]

This part of *The Wealth of Nations* has been much criticised as a 'labour theory' of value, which in turn allowed Karl Marx to claim that the labour of the workers was routinely stolen by the capitalist bosses. If so, it certainly did the world no good.

Yet Smith is not really leading us to a labour theory of value. He is actually trying to understand what today we see as a key economic measure, the *total costs of production*. In the hunting society, these costs are almost entirely labour. But we have evolved away from this; and Smith goes on to identify the other *factors of production* – land and capital – that are employed in more modern economic systems. This idea again has become a fundamental concept in economics today. And later, Smith brings in supply and demand, examining not just their effects on price, but how they drive the whole production and distribution system. It is pioneering stuff and it takes him several chapters, which need to be taken together, and which trace how society evolved away from labour as the sole source of value.[12]

Land, labour and capital

For modern production of any kind you need people to do the

---

10   Ibid., Book I, ch. VI, p. 65, para. 1.

11   Ibid., Book I, ch. V, p. 49, para. 4.

12   Ibid., Book I, chs V–XI.

work, equipment such as tools and machinery for them to do it with and space in which to work. Total costs can therefore be divided between *three broad factors of production*, asserts Smith.[13] Unlike in the hunting economy, these factors are owned by different people, who are therefore entitled to a share in the earnings from what is produced. There is the *labour* of the workers, of course, reflected in *wages*. There is also the *capital* (Smith says *stock*) put up by the employers, reflected in *profits*. And there is the use of *land*, reflected in the *rents* paid to landlords.

Land, capital and labour therefore all contribute to production, making workers, employers and landlords all interdependent. But their mutual dependency goes beyond mere production; since much production is intended for exchange, they are crucially involved in the valuation and distribution of that product too. Smith is leading us gradually to the realisation that the production, valuation and distribution of the nation's output do not exist in isolation, but all take place simultaneously as interrelated parts of a functioning economic *system*, of which everyone is a part. That too was a huge theoretical innovation.

How markets drive production

Smith then explains how this system *drives and directs production*. The 'market price' at which products actually exchange, he says, may be higher or lower than their total production cost (which he calls the 'natural price').[14] It depends on the demand for the product (or at least, the 'effectual' demand of customers with the money to buy) and on how much of it is brought to market. If the

---

13   Ibid., Book I, ch. VI.
14   Ibid., Book I, ch. VII.

market price is higher than sellers' total production costs, they make a profit; if it is lower, they make a loss.

The market price can never remain below production costs for long: sellers would withdraw, rather than suffer persistent losses. But nor can it long be very much higher. That would alert competitors that there are profits to be made; supply would increase and the market price would be bid down again. So industry's aim is to bring exactly the equilibrium amount to market.

Of course, competition may be imperfect. Regulations may restrict market entry. A monopolist may force up prices by keeping the market understocked. Or information may be deficient: for example, the inventor of a cheaper production process may enjoy extraordinary profits for years, until competitors also discover it. So 'natural' and market prices may diverge.

Wages depend on economic growth

Such imperfections exist in the *labour market* too. Land, capital and labour may be interdependent, but the struggle between workers and employers and landowners is an unequal one. Employers promote laws forbidding collusion between workers, says Smith, although collusion between employers is 'constant and uniform'.[15] But employers should remember that keeping wages low is a false economy: better pay and conditions can raise productivity and so generate higher returns.

The workers' best friends, he surmises, are rising national income and capital growth, because they bid up wages. A landlord with surplus revenue will hire more servants. A weaver or a

---

15   Ibid., Book I, ch. VIII, p. 84, para. 13.

shoemaker with surplus capital will hire assistants. In other words, the demand for labour rises when − and only when − national wealth rises. The 'liberal reward of labour' depends entirely on economic growth.

Yet the real measure of wages is how much they will buy; and Smith notes that while taxes had raised the price of candles, leather, alcohol and other luxuries of his time, food and other essentials were all getting cheaper, thanks to the market system. That helped the poor in particular, which was no bad thing, since: 'No society can surely be flourishing and happy, of which the far greater part of the members are poor and miserable.'[16]

Market wage rates

In theory, Smith ventures, the returns from labour should tend to equalise. If one trade were better rewarded, people would flock in from other professions and the market would soon correct the balance. So why do wage rates actually differ?

His answer is that we must look not just at the 'pecuniary' rewards, but the non-monetary rewards of labour too. Some professions are hard or disagreeable (which is why butchers and executioners are better paid than weavers). Some trades (like bricklaying) are seasonal. Others (such as medicine) command a premium because they require great public trust. Some professions are costly to learn (the law, for example); and even after such investment, the chance of real success might be slim (opera singers). All these factors will affect the market price of labour in particular trades.

---

16   Ibid., Book I, ch. VIII, p. 96, para. 36.

Wages and politics

But *political* factors affect incomes and profits too. Regulations prevent people from entering particular professions. Smith cites by-laws that forbid Sheffield cutlers from having more than one apprentice, or Norfolk weavers and English hatters more than two. These entry barriers keep up the incomes of the few who qualify as master cutlers, weavers and hatters – but only by robbing other people of the 'sacred property' of their own labour. And they prevent workers migrating from declining trades into ones where they are needed more.

Smith famously asserts that: 'People of the same trade seldom meet together, even for merriment and diversion, but the conversation ends in a conspiracy against the public, or in some contrivance to raise prices.'[17]

But (he continues immediately) politicians and the law are complicit, since they pass and enforce the regulations that make such collusion more likely and more effective. He has in mind the sort of privileges enjoyed by the craft guilds (or 'incorporations'), which, since the Middle Ages, had guarded jealously their own monopolies, restricted who could join the profession and on what terms, kept registers of those they licensed to practise and raised funds from members for the welfare of their own poor.

But a law establishing a public register of a profession's members, says Smith, puts them in easy contact with each other and so makes these conspiratorial meetings more likely to happen. Compulsory trade welfare funds make such meetings inevitable, since members of the profession have to come in to pay their levies. And where the law goes farther, allowing professions

---

17   Ibid., Book I, ch. X, part II, p. 145, para. 27.

to decide policy on a majority vote, it 'will limit the competition more effectually and more durably than any voluntary combination whatever'.[18]

To Smith, the only 'real and effectual' discipline over businesses is the fear of losing customers.[19] A free market in which customers are sovereign is a surer way to regulate business behaviour than any number of official rules – which so often produce the opposite of their avowed intention.

Capital and profits

Equally perverse regulations also affect the next factor of production, which Smith calls *stock*.[20] This, as he explains later,[21] includes goods reserved for immediate use, such as clothes or stocks of food; fixed capital, such as machinery; and circulating capital, including work in progress and goods that have been made but are still on the shelf.

Smith comments that the profit of stock – that is, the return to those who invest in productive enterprises – is very variable. It depends on commodity prices, on how competitors are faring and 'a thousand other accidents' that can happen to goods when they are being transported or stored.[22] Interest rates, however, provide a rough measure of profitability: if people are willing to pay a lot to borrow money, it suggests that they can make a handsome profit when they apply those borrowed funds to production.

By way of illustration, he points to the very high interest rates

18   Ibid., Book I, ch. X, part II, p. 145, para. 30.
19   Ibid., Book I, ch. X, part II, p. 146, para. 31.
20   Ibid., Book I, ch. X.
21   Ibid., Book II, ch. I.
22   Ibid., Book I, ch. IX, p. 105, para. 3.

pertaining in the American colonies, where there is abundant land, but relatively little capital or labour to cultivate it. Land is therefore cheap but capital and labour expensive – as reflected in high profits, high interest rates and high wages.

Land and rents

Smith's views on land and rents[23] show that he loves landlords no more than he loves employers: they enjoy a 'monopoly price' not through effort, but through the mere ownership of land and its location and fertility. Moreover, the desire of wealthy merchants to own impressive country estates increases the demand for land, and therefore land prices and rents, even more.

Land provides minerals as well as food and space, of course. Smith's long *Digression on Silver* assembles a mass of evidence to support his thesis that as national income grows manufactures get cheaper, but land gets more expensive.

An automatic system

To recapitulate: a country's 'annual produce' resolves itself into rent, wages and profits, meaning that landowners, workers and employers are inevitably interdependent.[24] They are parts of a seamless system of flows in which goods are created, exchanged, used and replaced – and resources are put to their best use – all quite automatically.

But the process can be perverted by vested interests, who use government power to distort this free market system for their

23   Ibid., Book I, ch. XI.
24   Ibid., Book I, ch. XI.

own benefit. Landowners may be too indolent and workers too powerless: but employers have both the incentive and the acuity to promote regulations that stifle competition. Therefore:

> The proposal of any new law or regulation of commerce which comes from this order, ought always to be listened to with great precaution, and ought never to be adopted till after having been long and carefully examined, not only with the most scrupulous, but with the most suspicious attention. It comes from an order of men, whose interest is never exactly the same with that of the public, who have generally an interest to deceive and even oppress the public, and who accordingly have, upon many occasions, both deceived and oppressed it.[25]

The accumulation of capital

Book II of *The Wealth of Nations* is about building up *capital*, which Smith asserts is an essential condition for economic progress. The creation of surpluses makes exchange and specialisation possible. This specialisation helps build even greater surpluses, which in turn can be reinvested in new, dedicated, labour-saving equipment. It is a virtuous circle. Thanks to this growth of capital, prosperity becomes an expanding pie: one person (or one nation) does not have to become poorer in order for another to become richer. On the contrary, as wealth expands, the whole nation becomes richer.

---

25 Ibid., Book I, ch. XI, p. 267, para. 10.

Money

Money, according to Smith, has no intrinsic value.[26] It is only a tool of exchange. Real wealth resides in what money buys, not in the coins themselves. After all, the purchasing power of gold and silver fluctuates. And a person who receives a guinea of income today may spend that same guinea tomorrow, thus providing the income of a second; and that person may spend the same guinea on the next day, providing the income of a third. So the amount of money in circulation is clearly not the same as the total income of the nation. The mercantilists are wrong to confuse the two.

Yet money does have its effects. When it lies around, it is a useless tool – 'dead stock' – but efficient banking can make it work harder. Today's fiat money (where governments simply declare the notes they print to be legal tender) did not exist in Smith's world, but banks issued notes backed by their gold reserves. This, he thought, could make it easier to keep cash moving, though he saw a risk if banks over-issued their notes – he was writing just after the 1772 banking crisis in which many Scottish banks collapsed. He thought that the threat of competition should keep the banks prudent, but still saw a role for banking regulation. (Smith is not against all economic regulation: only that designed to promote particular interests over the general welfare.)

Consumption and investment

Smith makes another innovative distinction, between gross and net income – total income minus the cost of achieving it.[27] Chapter III, on labour and savings, continues the analysis and is a core

---

26   Ibid., Book II, ch. II.
27   Ibid., Book II, ch. II.

part of *The Wealth of Nations*, though its terminology can confuse modern readers. Smith divides labour into *productive* and *unproductive*. By *productive labour* he means work that exceeds its costs and produces a surplus that is available for reinvestment – such as the labour of manufacturing staff. By *unproductive labour* he means work that is consumed immediately, like that of doctors or musicians, lawyers or puppeteers, public officials or buffoons, and which does not produce revenue that can be reinvested. He is making the distinction, so basic to economics today, between the manufacturing and service sectors.

By consuming these immediate services, however, we leave ourselves less surplus to invest in the maintenance and expansion of the capital on which our future income depends. The more we consume now, the more future growth and income must we forgo.

In fact, we can consume so much that we have nothing left with which to expand our productive capacity; so much, indeed, that we cannot even *maintain* it. That amounts to *consuming* our capital – as a 'prodigal' does, says Smith, by 'not confining his expense within his income', but paying 'the wages of idleness with those funds which the frugality of his forefathers … consecrated to the maintenance of industry'.[28]

Capital can also be dissipated by bad investment decisions (what Smith calls 'misconduct'). This, he reminds the mercantilists, does not diminish the nation's gold and silver deposits, but certainly reduces its productive capacity. And if there is no rule of law, capital can be stolen – reducing people's incentive to accumulate it in the first place.

28   Ibid., Book II, ch. II, p. 339, para. 20.

But 'great nations are never impoverished by private, though they sometimes are by public prodigality and misconduct'.[29] Ordinary people know that they must save and invest if they are to better themselves. Governments, however, have less focus on the importance of maintaining capital: their role is to spend on current services, not to invest in production. Almost the whole revenue of governments, observes Smith, is thus employed in maintaining *unproductive* hands. So:

> It is the highest impertinence and presumption … in kings and ministers, to pretend to watch over the economy of private people. … They are themselves always, and without any exception, the greatest spendthrifts in the society. … If their own extravagance does not ruin the state, that of their subjects never will.[30]

A 'profusion of government' may force taxpayers to 'encroach upon their capitals' until 'all the frugality and good conduct of individuals may not be able to compensate the waste and degradation of produce' that results. But the market economy remains a powerfully robust system. Big government may set nations back, but it can rarely stop them:

> The uniform, constant, and uninterrupted effort of every man to better his condition … is frequently powerful enough to maintain the natural progress of things toward improvement, in spite of both the extravagance of government, and of the greatest errors of administration.[31]

---

29 Ibid., Book II, ch. III. p. 342, para. 30.
30 Ibid., Book II, ch. III, p. 346, para. 36.
31 Ibid., Book II, ch. III, p. 343, para. 31.

Further reflections on capital

Smith observes that capital can be used in different ways.[32] Some assets (such as fisheries) provide for immediate consumption; others (like machinery) are used for manufacturing or transporting raw and finished goods; and, often ignored but equally important and productive, retail capital is used to break goods down into smaller, consumable units – so that when we want meat we do not need to buy a whole ox.

(This propels Smith into an amusing aside on official measures to restrict the number of retailers in any place, such as licensing ale-houses. 'It is not the multitude of ale-houses,' he says, 'that occasions a general disposition to drunkenness … but that disposition … necessarily gives employment to a multitude of ale-houses.'[33] Retail trades, like any other, follow demand.)

The core message of Book II, however, is that saving part of our product, instead of consuming it all, allows us to grow our productive capital; which in turn allows us to increase our product in the future. It is an expanding circle of wealth – unrelated (mercantilists please note) to the quantity of metal in our bank vaults.

Through the accumulation of capital, more specialist and more labour-saving processes can be developed. The division of labour will be deepened, which in turn, says Smith, will require more labour. As capital expands, therefore, wages will rise. (Smith was of course writing before the full force of the Industrial Revolution had become apparent and at a time when manual labour was fundamental to the economy. He does not seem to imagine machines actually replacing labour.)

In other words, the market economy is unparalleled at

32   Ibid., Book II, ch. V.
33   Ibid., Book II, ch. V, p. 360, para. 7.

boosting national wealth, and this wealth diffuses right down to the poorest workers. Indeed, the poor in the rich countries that adopt this system live better than the rich in the poor countries that do not. It is a globalisation message: countries make themselves better off if they do not try to remain self-sufficient or raise trade barriers against others.

The history of economic institutions

Book III looks at the development of economic relations, sometimes through historical conjecture, sometimes through a wealth of historical fact. Smith begins by tracing the evolution from agriculture to industry. The growth of towns, and the interdependence of towns and the countryside, is entirely natural, he asserts. Artisans need farmers to produce their food, but farmers need artisans to make their equipment, and towns to provide markets for their goods: indeed, the larger the town, the bigger the market. It is not (as the French 'physiocrat' economists of the time contended) that the towns simply live off the country: both sides add value from the exchange of their different contributions.

Smith charts the breakdown of the feudal order in Europe and explores the origins of feudal law after the fall of the Roman Empire and how commerce led to it being supplanted.[34] Before the age of trade and commerce, he speculates, wealth resided with the great landlords; and these barons inevitably became the local legal authorities too. It was an arbitrary power, however, and feudal law developed as an attempt to moderate it – though with only partial success. But the rise of trade and commerce saw the wealth

---

34   Ibid., Book III, ch. IV.

(and thus the power) of the landowners being eroded and their retainers becoming independent tenants. Those tenants, now with aspirations of their own, demanded more security, and the feudal system gave way to a rule of law that applied to the great and the humble alike. The rise of commerce had separated economic from political power: and economic power is powerful indeed.

This was a happy outcome, in Smith's opinion, because it protected people's capital and allowed trade, commerce and manufactures to grow under the shelter of civil justice. Once again, a beneficial outcome was brought about by groups of people who had not the least intention of serving the general public, but were mindful only of their own property and security.

Economic theory and policy

In Book IV, Smith builds his critique of economic interventionism. He starts with mercantilism and its erroneous view that money and wealth are the same things – and its policy to restrict imports and expand exports so as to hold on to as much gold and silver as possible.[35]

Mercantilists and money

Money, Smith reminds us, is just a tool to facilitate exchange. Since foreign trade is a small part of total commerce, cross-border movements of gold are hardly likely to ruin a great nation.

Of course, the mercantilists say that gold is durable and that the countries that export to us could viciously accumulate it over

---

35   Ibid., Book IV, ch. I.

decades while we stupidly exchange perishable commodities for such a durable one. Smith retorts that we are perfectly happy to import (perishable) wines from France and export (durable) hardware in return. But the French are not so silly as to accumulate more pots and pans than they really need; and nor should we be so stupid as to hoard gold and silver beyond their useful quantities. An excess of inert metal is dead capital, and dead capital cannot make us rich.

Absolute advantage

When we restrict imports in the hope of preserving our gold and silver deposits, Smith continues, it means that domestic consumers have less choice: they have to buy from home producers, rather than from a range of foreign producers whose goods may be better or cheaper.[36] This makes the policy expensive and counterproductive. As with the division of labour between trades, countries too should do what they are best at and exchange their surpluses. This argument is an early rendition of the principle that today we call *absolute advantage*, and Smith seals the case with a vivid example:

> By means of glasses, hotbeds and hotwalls, very good grapes can be raised in Scotland, and very good wine too can be made of them at about thirty times the expense for which at least equally good can be brought from foreign countries. Would it be a reasonable law to prohibit the importation of all foreign wines, merely to encourage the making of claret and burgundy in Scotland?[37]

36 Ibid., Book IV, ch. II.
37 Ibid., Book IV, ch. II, p. 458, para. 15.

Such interventionism is not only irrational and expensive. It is also corrupting:

> The statesman, who should attempt to direct private people
> in what manner they ought to employ their capitals, would
> not only load himself with a most unnecessary attention,
> but assume an authority which could safely be trusted,
> not only to no single person, but to no council or senate
> whatever, and which would nowhere be so dangerous as in
> the hands of a man who had folly and presumption enough
> to fancy himself fit to exercise it.[38]

Tariffs and subsidies

There might, Smith concedes, be a case for *temporary* tariffs if they forced other countries to drop theirs. But in general such policies are either pointless or harmful and we should be suspicious of people who advocate them. British tariffs on foreign wine and beer, for example, are defended on the grounds that they reduce drunkenness. But, Smith retorts, though alcohol may sometimes be abused, it is still better if we can buy it more cheaply than we can brew it ourselves. He notes also that the tariffs favour Portugal over France, on the argument that Portugal is a better customer for British manufactures. 'The sneaking arts of underling tradesmen', he complains, 'are thus erected into political maxims for the conduct of a great empire.'[39]

Nor should we necessarily worry about an adverse balance of trade, Smith tells the mercantilists. As long as a country is producing more than it consumes, it is saving and adding to its

---

38   Ibid., Book IV, ch. II, p. 456, para. 10.
39   Ibid., Book IV, ch. III, part II, p. 493, para. c8.

capital. Such a country could still import more than it exports and nevertheless continue to produce surpluses and grow richer.

Smith's review of other trade interventions, including 'drawbacks' (tax reliefs for exporters) and 'bounties' (subsidies),[40] provides an interesting snapshot of his period, and there is the occasional, telling gem. For example:

> The bounty to the white-herring fishery is a tonnage bounty;
> and is proportioned to the burden of the ship, not to her
> diligence or success in the fishery; and it has, I am afraid,
> been too common for vessels to fit out for the sole purpose
> of catching, not the fish, but the bounty.[41]

Colonial trade restrictions

The Wealth of Nations was published just months before America's seething discontents turned into outright rebellion. Smith's chapter on colonies[42] reveals his sympathy with the Americans, mainly on account of the mercantilist restrictions that have harmed their trade (and done Britain no good in the process) and partly because he feels that America's contribution to tax revenues should, as a matter of justice, entitle it to greater representation in Parliament.

Tracing the origins of colonies, Smith suggests that they are usually established with the hope of finding gold or silver, which of course the mercantilists equate with wealth. But America's great asset is land. It is plentiful and cheap, and much labour is needed to realise its potential yield. That makes labour expensive, but

40   Ibid., Book IV, chs IV and V.

41   Ibid., Book IV, ch. V, p. 520, para. 32.

42   Ibid., Book IV, ch. VII.

American agriculture is in fact so productive that labour remains affordable nonetheless. Indeed, America is so fertile and rich that even Britain's taxes and trade restrictions have not (yet) ruined it.

Unfortunately, the policy of forcing America to trade only with the home country has drawn Britain's capital and enterprise away from more productive uses – depressing its prosperity along with America's, and leading to slower capital accumulation and therefore lower future incomes in both. Britain, he says, has tried to make America 'a people of customers', but the policy instead has turned them from farmers into politicians: and since so much of Britain's industry is focused on the Atlantic trade, the political risk is large. Only trade – and political – liberalisation could reduce the threat, but Britain's investment has become so distorted that the necessary adjustment would be painful.

Britain's trade restrictions on America are yet another example of mercantilist thinking, where producer interests dominate. But: 'Consumption is the sole end and purpose of all production; and the interest of the producer ought to be attended to, only so far as it may be necessary for promoting that of the consumer.'[43]

The liberal alternative

Smith criticises the French physiocrats for their view that all value derives from land and agriculture – the town merchants and 'artificers' merely rearranging this wealth, but producing nothing themselves. He counters that the townspeople are in fact productive. They do not simply consume capital: they replace it. They are *productive*, not *unproductive* hands.

---

43   Ibid., Book IV, ch. VIII, p. 660, para. 49.

He nevertheless considers the physiocrats' economic philosophy as one of the better ones. They do not mistake output for money and they see perfect freedom of trade as the best way to maximise that output.

Smith holds that the market economy is strong enough to survive, even if freedom is less than perfect: but the joy of a free economic system is that it works automatically. In Smith's words, the 'obvious and simple system of natural liberty establishes itself of its own accord'. People are left free to pursue their own interests – and thereby, as we have seen, they unwittingly promote the interests of everyone. No central direction is needed:

> The sovereign is completely discharged from a duty [for which] no human wisdom or knowledge could ever be sufficient; the duty of superintending the industry of private people, and of directing it towards the employments most suitable to the interest of the society.[44]

Which is fortunate in Smith's view, since every system that tries to steer resources in particular directions 'is in reality subversive of the great purpose which it means to promote'.[45]

The role of government

Smith explores the proper role of government in Book V. He is critical of government and officialdom, but is no champion of laissez-faire. He believes that the market economy he has described can function and deliver its benefits only when its rules are observed – when property is secure and contracts are

---

44   Ibid., Book IV, ch. IX, p. 687, para. 51.
45   Ibid., Book IV, ch. IX, p. 687, para. 50.

honoured. The maintenance of *justice* and *the rule of law* are therefore vital.

So is *defence*. If our property can be stolen by a foreign power, we are no better off than if our own neighbours steal it.

But Smith goes farther than this and argues that there is also a role for the government in *providing public works* and *promoting education*.

Defence

Smith conjectures that in a world of hunter-gatherers, everyone must defend themselves. But since hunters live for the day and have little or no property, there is little call for any central authority. In an agricultural age, however, people start to accumulate valuable property (crops and livestock, for example) and defending it becomes a priority. Under the division of labour principle, a specialist military is established. Those with most property have most to gain, but they compel everyone to contribute rather than remain 'free riders'. So defence has become a function of government.

Justice

The same historical argument applies to justice. As people move to a commercial, exchange society, those with property establish civil government to defend themselves against their neighbours who have none:

> The affluence of the rich excites the indignation of the poor,

who are often both driven by want, and prompted by envy, to invade his possessions. It is only under the shelter of the civil magistrate that the owner of that valuable property, which is acquired by the labour of many years, or perhaps of many successive generations, can sleep a single night in security.[46]

It is obviously useful if everyone accepts the authority of independent judges. But the efforts of the rich and powerful to build a judicial shelter for themselves are abetted by a natural human tendency to respect the authority of personal qualities such as strength, wisdom, prudence, maturity, wealth and status.

Civil government, in other words, is the outcome of conflict and of the inequalities that emerge in a commercial society. It is a natural outcome, a generally helpful one, but is by no means perfect.

Civil government, so far as it is instituted for the security of property, is in reality instituted for the defence of the rich against the poor, or of those who have some property against those who have none at all.[47]

It is no surprise that the structure of government, having been built on these imperfect foundations, is imperfect too. The power to tax allows it to build up enormous resources, but it has much less incentive to manage its property as efficiently as would a private individual. Thus:

When the crown lands had become private property, they would, in the course of a few years, become well-improved and well-cultivated … the revenue which the crown derives from the duties of customs and excise, would

---

46 Ibid., Book V, ch. I, part II, p. 710, para. c2.
47 Ibid., Book V, ch. I, part II, p. 715, para. 12.

necessarily increase with the revenue and consumption of
the people.[48]

This lack of incentive must be corrected: 'Public services are
never better performed than when their reward comes in consequence of their being performed, and is proportioned to the diligence employed in performing them.'[49]

Public works and institutions

Smith's third duty of government is 'the duty of erecting and
maintaining certain public works and certain public institutions,
which it can never be for the interest of any individual, or small
number of individuals, to erect and maintain'.[50]

These comprise *infrastructure projects* that facilitate commerce
and *education*, which helps make people a constructive part of the
social and economic order.

Public works

Prosperity requires commerce and commerce needs infrastructure, such as roads, bridges and harbours. Some of these, Smith
believes, could never repay their cost, and tax funding is needed
to build them. But at least part of the cost could be recovered
by tolls on those who use them, rather than by taxes upon the
whole nation. Likewise, if the main benefit is local and the
cost cannot be recovered by tolls, a *local* tax is best: London

---

48 Ibid., Book V, ch. II, part I, p. 824, para. a18.
49 Ibid., Book V, ch. I, part II, p. 719, para. 20.
50 Ibid., Book IV, ch. I, part III, p. 723, para. c1.

taxpayers should pay for paving and streetlights in London, for example.

Smith also sees the need for public concessions to encourage people to open up trade with 'barbarous' countries. But this help should be given in the form of temporary local monopolies (such as patents or copyright) rather than subsidies from the general taxpayer.

Since *The Wealth of Nations* up to this point has been an extended condemnation of governments 'directing the capitals' of the people, these public expenditure proposals seem odd at best. Commerce certainly requires infrastructure, just as it requires rules of justice. It is not obvious, however, why roads, bridges and harbours should not be built commercially and the cost recovered entirely by charges on their users. Even paving and streetlights might be installed and paid for by local businesses, which could gain trade as a result. And if it is worth opening up new trade routes, why does the government need to be involved?

Perhaps we can excuse Smith on the grounds that today we have much more extensive financial instruments to provide the funding for new trade ventures and for laying down essential infrastructure. We also have better technologies for collecting payments from those who use roads, bridges and other facilities. But in the eighteenth century, government funding and initiative seemed the only way of doing certain things that everyone agreed were essential.

The education of youth
Smith sees the promotion of basic education as akin to infrastructure – something needed in order to allow commerce to thrive.

But here again, his analysis and prescriptions seem inconsistent with his general analysis.

His starting point is that, for all its benefits, the division of labour may have undesirable social consequences. The daily focus on repetitive tasks inevitably narrows people's views and interests:

> The man whose whole life is spent in performing a few
> simple operations, of which the effects too are, perhaps,
> always the same, or very nearly the same, has no occasion
> to exert his understanding, or to exercise his invention in
> finding out expedients for removing difficulties which never
> occur.[51]

Marx would later call it 'alienation' and Smith insists that education is needed to correct it. Education should focus on the labouring poor, who suffer most (manufacturers and traders live in a more stimulating world). And to facilitate commerce, says Smith, people need to 'read, write, and account'; geometry and mechanics are also useful.

The 'public' can facilitate this education by establishing schools – such as the local government-funded school that Smith went to in Kirkcaldy. But while the state might pay for school buildings, it should not pay the whole of teachers' wages. If teachers rely on fees from students, their performance will be that much sharper. Smith recalls with irritation his time in Oxford, where: 'The endowments of schools and colleges have necessarily diminished more or less the necessity of application in the teachers. Their subsistence [is] altogether independent of their success and reputation in their particular professions.'[52]

51 Ibid., Book V, ch. I, part III, p. 782, para. f50.
52 Ibid., Book V, ch. I, part III, article II, p. 760, para. f5.

He remains unclear on just how much the government should pay towards this basic education, though he expresses high regard for the private schools for skills like fencing or dancing, where the students pay the whole amount. But mindful of Smith's warnings about government enterprises, a modern reader might ask whether it is not better to subsidise needy students rather than their schools.

Education for all ages

Smith also sees a role for the government in promoting adult and religious education. Churchmen grow lazy when tithes pay their salaries, but the temptations of the growing towns mean that religious and moral education has never been more important. So he advocates at least some role for the government in encouraging the study of science, philosophy and the arts – though again, without being specific. And, he argues, a government should give 'serious attention' to combating the 'mental mutilation' of cowardice, just as it should prevent the spread of 'leprosy or any other loathsome and offensive disease'.[53]

The sovereign

A last item that should be paid out of taxation is maintaining the 'dignity of the sovereign', which includes the costs of the monarchy and criminal justice. But much *civil* justice should be paid by the protagonists in disputes, he maintains, since it is they who derive the principal benefit.

---

53 Ibid., Book V, ch. I, part III, article II, pp. 787–8, para. f60.

The principles of taxation

Having established that at least some taxation is necessary, Smith turns to the question of how best to raise it. Here he is on more familiar and secure ground. He is fully aware that: 'There is no art which one government sooner learns of another than that of draining money from the pockets of the people.'[54]

Plainly, then, some restraint is needed, and Smith proposes four famous principles of taxation. First, people should contribute in proportion to the income that they enjoy under the security of state protection. Second, taxes ought to be certain, rather than depend on the arbitrary decisions of tax officers. Third, tax should not be inconvenient to pay. Fourth, taxes should have minimal side effects: they should be cheap to collect; they should not hamper industry and enterprise; they should not be so onerous as to encourage evasion, such as smuggling; and they should not require 'frequent visits and the odious examination of the tax-gatherers'.[55]

Taxation is something that governments have to get right, says Smith. A tax on companies is unwise, for example, because – as he observes with great insight – the capital on which our income depends is highly mobile:

> The proprietor of stock is properly a citizen of the world, and is not necessarily attached to any particular country. He would be apt to abandon the country in which he was exposed to a vexatious inquisition, in order to be assessed to a burdensome tax, and would remove his stock to some other country where he could either carry on his business, or enjoy his fortune more at his ease.[56]

54 Ibid., Book V, ch. II, part II, appendix to articles I and II, p. 861, para. h12.
55 Ibid., Book V, ch. II, part II, p. 827, para. b6.
56 Ibid., Book V, ch. II, article II, pp. 848–9, para. f8.

But there are inconsistencies in Smith's plans here too. He opposes taxes on consumption, but supports a tax on luxuries (including things that we would think rather basic today, such as poultry). He says that people should pay tax in proportion to their income, but wants the rich to pay 'something more than in that proportion'.

Public debts

While some of Smith's views on the role of government seem inconsistent with his general principles, and his policy prescriptions seem not to be thought through with his usual precision, he finishes in something more like his old style. Governments, he notes, have a tendency to spend even more than they can drain out of the pockets of the people. So he ends *The Wealth of Nations* with the parting warning that a large national debt is particularly harmful.[57]

By issuing debt, governments draw capital away from investment and growth, and steer it towards present consumption – in the shape of government activities – which means that growth necessarily falters. In addition, government borrowing allows politicians to take on more functions and boost their own power, without having to ask the people for more tax. And they often find ways of avoiding repayments anyway. For these reasons, national debt is not just a benign transfer from one group to another: it is a real threat to liberty and therefore a real threat to prosperity.

---

57   Ibid., Book V, ch. III.

The Wealth of Nations today

Smith's world was very different to ours, of course, before the Industrial Revolution changed everything. He was suspicious of the joint-stock companies that are the mainstay of capitalism today, arguing that 'an immense number of proprietors' could never keep them focused.[58] Perhaps he was right. He did not forecast the rise of union power, the problems of industrial pollution, fiat money inflation and much else that troubles economists today.

And yet, by showing how the freedom and security to work, trade, save and invest promotes our prosperity, without the need for a directing authority, *The Wealth of Nations* still leaves us with a powerful set of solutions to the worst economic problems that the world can throw at us. The free economy is an adaptable and flexible system, which can withstand the shock of the new and cope with whatever the future brings.

---

58   Ibid., Book V, ch. I, part II, article I, p. 744, para. e22.

4   *THE THEORY OF MORAL SENTIMENTS*

The Theory of Moral Sentiments was published in 1759, when Adam Smith was 35, and came out of his lecture course on Ethics at the University of Glasgow. It is not an easy book to read – Smith also lectured on Rhetoric and Literary Style, and the language is more ornate than the clipped scientific prose of philosophers today. Indeed, Smith's friend Edmund Burke described it as 'rather painting than writing'. It needs to be read slowly.

Main themes of the book

Yet *The Theory of Moral Sentiments* was a real scientific breakthrough. It shows that our moral ideas and actions are a product of very nature as social creatures. It argues that this social psychology is a better guide to moral action than reason. It identifies the basic rules of *prudence* and *justice* that are needed for society to survive and explains the additional, *beneficent*, actions that enable it to flourish.

Self-interest and sympathy

As individuals we have a natural tendency to look after ourselves. That is merely prudence. And yet as *social* creatures, explains Smith, we are also endowed with a natural *sympathy* towards others. (Today this word has acquired other meanings and *empathy* might express the concept better.) When we see others distressed or happy, we feel for them – albeit less strongly. Likewise, others seek our empathy and feel for us. But when their feelings are particularly strong, empathy prompts them to restrain their emotions so as to bring them into line with our less intense reactions. Gradually, as we grow from childhood to adulthood, we each learn what is and is not acceptable to other people. Morality stems from our social nature.

Justice and beneficence

So does justice. Though we are self-interested, we again have to work out how to live alongside others without doing them harm. That is an essential minimum for the survival of society. If people go farther and do positive good – beneficence – we welcome it, but we cannot *demand* such action as we demand justice.

Virtue

Prudence, justice and beneficence are important. The ideal must be, however, that any impartial person, real or imaginary – what Smith calls an *impartial spectator* – would fully empathise with our emotions and actions. That requires *self-command* and in this lies true virtue.

Natural empathy as the basis of virtue

Philosophers of Smith's time were looking for rational explanations of what made actions right or wrong. But Smith thought that our morality is not so calculating. Rather, it is something natural, built into us as social beings. We each feel sympathy (or empathy) with others[1] which is immediate, genuine, benevolent and natural. In our imagination, we see ourselves in the position of others. If we see someone about to be struck, we wince; when we gaze at a performer on a slack rope, we writhe along with them. And when we see people happy or sad, we feel happy or sad too.

Similarly, we empathise when we see people acting in ways we approve of. In fact, we feel genuine pleasure from sharing in the emotions and opinions of others.[2] And when we do not share the emotions of others, or disapprove of their actions, it is mutually distressing.

It is, however, not so much the emotion itself that we empathise with, says Smith, but the situation that gave rise to it. When we see an angry person, we are more likely to fear for the potential victims of this anger than to share in it, at least until we have learnt the facts of the case and have made our own judgement as to how far the anger is justified. If we feel that people have overreacted to some incident, they lose our empathy.

Discord and self-restraint

Smith notes that, as mere spectators, we cannot fully share the ferocity of other people's emotions – the fierce anger of someone who has been wronged, for example, or the profound grief of someone recently bereaved. Our empathic emotion, though genuine, is inevitably weaker. But other people are spectators of our emotions, just as we are of theirs. Where there is discordance

---

1   *The Theory of Moral Sentiments*, part I, section I, ch. I, p. 9, para. 1.

2   Ibid., part I, section I, ch. II.

between their feelings and ours, as in these cases, they will feel distress. This in turn will prompt them to restrain the violence of their original feelings in order to bring themselves more into line with our view of their predicament.

As we make our way through life, we learn this self-restraint. By our nature, we see things from other people's point of view and we learn that an excess of anger or grief or other emotions distresses them. So we try to curb our emotions to bring them into line with those of others. In fact, we aim to temper them to the point where any typical, disinterested person – an *impartial spectator*, says Smith – would empathise with us.

Likewise, when we show concern for other people, we know that an impartial spectator would approve and we take pleasure from it. The impartial spectator may be real or only imaginary, but still guides us: and through experience we gradually build up a system of behavioural norms – morality. This helps society to flourish. And at its root is empathy:

> And hence it is, that to feel much for others and little for ourselves, that to restrain our selfish, and to indulge our benevolent affections, constitutes the perfection of human nature; and can alone produce among mankind that harmony of sentiments and passions in which consists their whole grace and propriety.[3]

Reward, punishment and society

Smith considers the appropriateness of various emotions such as hunger, love, kindness and resentment[4] then turns to the question of what behaviour merits reward or punishment.

---

3   Ibid., part I, section I, ch. V, p. 25, para. 5.
4   Ibid., part I, section II.

To form a judgement on this, he tells us, we need to separate results from motives. If one person benefits from the helpful action of another, we cannot fully empathise with the beneficiary's gratitude unless the agent acted from motives that we agree with. Nor can we empathise with someone's resentment of a harmful action unless the action stemmed from motives we disapprove of.[5] Only when a helpful action stems from a positive motive do we believe it merits reward; and only when a harmful action stems from a negative motive do we believe it merits punishment.[6]

Punishments and rewards have an important social function. We approve of and reward acts that benefit society, and disapprove of and punish acts that harm it: 'The very existence of society requires that unmerited and unprovoked malice should be restrained by proper punishments; and consequently, that to inflict those punishments should be regarded as a proper and laudable action.'[7]

This process is instinctive: we may not know exactly how individual actions bring about the benefit or harm of society, and our reason is an uncertain guide. But nature, or God, has equipped us with appetites and aversions that do in fact seem to promote the continued existence of our species and our society. Indeed, if we behaved otherwise, society would fracture and we as social creatures would soon cease to exist.

This is an example of what Smith has in mind on the few occasions when he talks about the 'invisible hand' and on the many more when he explains how our actions serve to produce a well-functioning social order, even though such an outcome is not our

---

5   Ibid., part II, section I, chs III and IV.

6   Ibid., part II, section I, ch. IV.

7   Ibid., part II, section I, ch. V, p. 77, para. 10.

purpose when we act. For example, the wheels of a watch work together to show the time, Smith observes. But they do not know that: it is the watchmaker's intention. Likewise, when our instinctive actions work to promote society, we may conceitedly ascribe it to our own reason, but really we should ascribe it to nature, or to God.[8]

(When he discusses this phenomenon of the functioning social order that is produced by human action but not human design, Smith uses the terms *God, Nature* or *the Author of Nature* almost interchangeably. But his explanation of how, through our actions, we unwittingly create social harmony is a systems approach, not a theological approach. It neither presumes nor requires the intervention of a deity. Nature – or, as we might say today, evolution – can produce the same outcome perfectly well.)

This brings us back to the question of motives.[9] Actions that are intended to harm may in fact not do so; while other actions can produce real harm even where none was intended. Should we then punish motives, or results? Smith answers that we cannot look into the human heart: if we punished only bad *motives*, nobody would be safe from suspicion. But again, nature leads us to a more stable solution: we punish only those *actions* that produce evil, or are intended to.

Justice as a foundation

For society to survive there must be rules to prevent its individual members harming each other. As Smith comments, it is possible for a society of robbers and murderers to exist – but only insofar

---

8   Ibid., part II, section II, ch. III.
9   Ibid., part II, section III, chs I and II.

as they abstain from robbing and murdering each other.[10] These are the rules we call justice.

If people do not help others when they could, or fail to return a good deed, we may call them uncharitable or ungrateful. But we do not punish people to force them to *do good*: only for acts of real or intended *harm*. We force them only to obey the rules of justice, because society could not otherwise survive.[11]

Justice is about preventing harm, not maximising good. We do not allow people to steal something from another, for example, merely because it may be of greater use to themselves.[12] Since everyone tends to think their own interests more important than those of everyone else, we would all face countless predations from others if we did. Justice is how society defends itself from harm, and it is so essential that nature has given us the strongest instincts to maintain it. Our disapproval of injustice is so strong that it provokes deep shame and remorse in those who are guilty of it.

Self-criticism and conscience

In fact, says Smith, nature has given us something even more immediate than punishment, namely our own self-criticism. We are impartial spectators, not only of other people's actions, but of our own too, dividing ourselves between agent and judge.[13] And this internal judge demands more than the mere praise of others: we want to be *worthy* of praise too, and are content

---

10   Ibid., part II, section II, ch. III, p. 86, para. 3.
11   Ibid., part II, section II, ch. I.
12   Ibid., part II, section II, ch. II.
13   Ibid., part III, ch. I.

only when we feel that other people's opinion of us is genuinely deserved.[14]

This spark of conscience, he maintains, has a powerful social function. It prevents us from becoming too absorbed in our own fate and too distant from the fate of others. In a famous example, he observes that if a great earthquake consumed the whole of China, a person living in Europe might feel some distress: but it would be nothing compared with the distress caused by some private misfortune:

> If he were to lose his little finger tomorrow, he would not
> sleep tonight; but, provided he never saw them, he will
> snore with the most profound security over the ruin of
> a hundred millions of his brethren, and the destruction
> of that immense multitude seems plainly an object less
> interesting to him, than this paltry misfortune of his own.[15]

In reality, though, all individuals are equally important. Conscience is nature's way of reminding us of that. Would we sacrifice the lives of hundreds of millions of people just to save our own little finger? Of course not: our conscience would never allow it. Conscience gives us perspective: it checks our self-obsession and makes us unwilling to harm others merely for our personal gain. It gives us self-command over our own base appetites.[16]

Moral rules

This process is supported by our natural instinct to make and to follow rules. When we see people behaving badly, says Smith, our

---

14   Ibid., part III, ch. II.
15   Ibid., part III, ch. III, pp. 136–7, para. 4.
16   Ibid., part III, ch. III.

internal judge makes us resolve not to do the same; and when others behave well, we resolve to emulate them. In the process of making such judgements on a countless number of actions, we gradually formulate rules of conduct.[17] That means we no longer have to think out each new situation afresh: we now have moral standards to guide us. They engender a 'sense of duty' that helps keep us true to the principles of justice, honesty and politeness, no matter how we might be feeling at the time.

This constancy is beneficial to the social order. By following our conscience, we end up, surely but unintentionally, promoting the happiness of mankind.[18] Human laws, with their punishments and rewards, may aim at the same results; but they can never be as consistent, immediate or effective as conscience and the rules of morality that are engineered by nature.

Smith concedes that moral rules do vary over time and place. Just as different cultures have different ideas of beauty, depending on what they are familiar with, they also have different ideas about the 'beauty of conduct'.[19] For example, there are differing marriage customs and norms of sexual conduct and differing standards of hospitality or politeness. But such differences of fashion or custom are inevitably marginal, he insists. Unless the fundamental principles of nature continue to be observed, society cannot continue to survive.

Attitudes to wealth

Another factor that can affect our moral judgements, and not all

---

17   Ibid., part III, ch. IV, p. 159, paras 7–8.
18   Ibid., part III, ch. V.
19   Ibid., part V, ch. I, and ch. II, p. 200, para. 1.

for the good, is wealth. Smith's lengthy reflections on this subject must come as a shock to naive critics who (following Karl Marx) imagine him as a champion of material acquisitiveness.

The material conveniences that money can buy are actually quite trifling, he insists. A fine coat is no more weatherproof than a rough one; a rich person can eat no more than anyone else; and the labourer in a humble cottage probably sleeps more soundly than a monarch in a great palace. Wealth cannot rescue us from fear, sorrow or death.

Yet we still believe that money can buy happiness and that the rich and famous must be happy. Indeed, we feel an empathic pleasure in their good fortune, and their lives and affairs capture our interest. Being the focus of public attention is, of course, very agreeable: so for the rich, the main benefit of wealth becomes not the trivial comforts it can buy, but the flattering interest that it generates.

This is vanity, however, because the public's interest depends more on the possession of wealth or status than on the merit of those who possess them. Even people with nothing to gain tend to overlook the 'vice and folly' of the wealthy and flatter them beyond their deserving. As a result, those with wealth or status come to think that they genuinely deserve all this false praise, even when they actually deserve none of it.

Self-improvement

And yet the pursuit of wealth does bring other benefits.[20] When people see the big houses or fine coaches of the rich, they envy this

---

20   Ibid., part IV, ch. I.

life of supposed comfort and ease. Paradoxically, says Smith, they will commit themselves to a lifetime of discomfort and hard work to achieve the same. In this way, the presumed pleasures of wealth – though in fact a delusion – drive us to make enormous exertions in our physical world and lead us into vast improvements in our intellectual and artistic lives too:

> It is this deception which rouses and keeps in continual motion the industry of mankind. It is this which first prompted them to cultivate the ground, to build houses, to found cities and commonwealths, and to invent and improve all the sciences and arts, which ennoble and embellish human life; which have entirely changed the whole face of the globe, have turned the rude forests of nature into agreeable and fertile plains, and made the trackless and barren ocean a new fund of subsistence, and the great high road of communication to the different nations of the earth.[21]

The rich, however, consume little more than the poor: they merely pick things that are more precious or agreeable or refined. And by giving employment to all those who wait on them or whose industry is needed to make all their fine trinkets, the wealth that they have acquired spreads out through the whole community. Indeed, they are 'led by an invisible hand to make nearly the same distribution of the necessaries of life, which would have been made, had the earth been divided into equal portions among its inhabitants'.[22]

---

21   Ibid., part IV, ch. I, pp. 183–4, para. 10.
22   Ibid., part IV, ch. I, pp. 184–5, para. 10.

On virtue

Having identified the origins and nature of morality, Smith ends *The Theory of Moral Sentiments* by defining the character of a truly virtuous person. Such a person, he suggests, would embody the qualities of *prudence, justice* and *beneficence*. A fourth – *self-command* – is also essential, though it is not always a force for good.

Prudence is directed at the care of the individual. It moderates the individual's excesses and as such is important for society. It is respectable, if not particularly endearing.[23] *Justice* is directed at limiting the harm we do to others. It is essential for the continuation of social life. *Beneficence* improves that social life by prompting us to promote the happiness of others. It cannot be demanded from anyone, but it is always appreciated. And *self-command* moderates our passions. (Fear may restrain our anger, but the anger simply re-emerges when we are safe again. But when, through self-command, we moderate our anger to be in empathy with others, it is genuinely reduced.[24])

We have a natural tendency to be most concerned about ourselves, then about our family, and only then about friends and more distant people.[25] We tend to have more regard for our own country than for others.[26] But true benevolence, argues Smith, knows no boundary. Since humanity is more important than any individual, a truly virtuous person should be willing to make personal sacrifices 'to the greater interest of the universe'.[27]

---

23   Ibid., part VI, section I, ch. I.
24   Ibid., part VI, Conclusion, p. 263, para. 3.
25   Ibid., part VI, section I, ch. I.
26   Ibid., part VI, section I, ch. II.
27   Ibid., part VI, section III, ch. III, p. 235, para. 3.

The constitution of a virtuous society

Nature does, in fact, prompt individuals into acts of self-sacrifice and we admire the self-command that allows them to commit such acts. But people can sacrifice themselves for bad causes as well as good. The self-command of the hero can turn into the steely determination of the zealot.

Affection for humankind is not the same as affection for our state.[28] That involves a respect and reverence for the constitution and organisation of the country, as well as a desire that our fellow citizens should be happy. Usually, those two things coincide. But in times of political turmoil, they can collide.

In such circumstances, politicians may resort to proposing sweeping plans for reform. They propose the overthrow of existing institutions, says Smith, regardless of the benefits that those old institutions have delivered. They propose instead a 'rational' alternative. But this is at odds with human nature:

> The man of system ... is apt to be very wise in his own
> conceit; and is often so enamoured with the supposed
> beauty of his own ideal plan of government, that he cannot
> suffer the smallest deviation from any part of it ... He seems
> to imagine that he can arrange the different members of a
> great society with as much ease as the hand arranges the
> different pieces upon a chess-board. He does not consider
> that in the great chess-board of human society, every
> single piece has a principle of motion of its own, altogether
> different from that which the legislature might choose to
> impress upon it.[29]

Freedom and nature are a surer guide to the creation of a

---

28 Ibid., part VI, section II, ch. II, p. 229, para. 4.
29 Ibid., part VI, section II, ch. II, pp. 233–4, para. 17.

harmonious, functioning society than the overweening reason of zealots and visionaries.

5 SMITH'S LECTURES AND OTHER WRITINGS

Smith ordered that most of his unpublished papers should be burnt at his death (quite a normal request at the time, when writers wanted to be judged on their finished work rather than on their rough notes). So beyond *The Wealth of Nations* and *The Theory of Moral Sentiments*, little of his written work survives. What there is, however, shows the enormous breadth of Smith's learning and interests: a review of Samuel Johnson's *Dictionary*; articles on intellectual trends in Europe and on the origin of languages; essays on the arts, covering painting, drama, music and dance; remarks on English and Italian poetry; papers on the history of ancient physics and philosophy; and a 70-page dissertation on *The History of Astronomy*.

Fortunately, we also have some of his students' notes from his *Lectures on Rhetoric and Belles Lettres* and *Lectures on Jurisprudence*. Although these are not Smith's written words, they give us valuable insights into his intellectual development at Glasgow, and many paragraphs reappear in *The Wealth of Nations*.

The unifying theme

Despite the great variety of subjects that Smith covers in these various lectures and writings, they all reveal one important thing about his approach. Smith is not so much an economist, or moralist, or historian, or grammarian, as a social psychologist. He wants to know how the human mind deals with the world and with other humans, and how it creates great things from these relationships. Science, to him, is less about reality than about how human minds analyse and arrange that reality for themselves. Language, morality and economics are all useful social structures that somehow emerge from the meeting of minds. Law and justice are about how human beings secure peaceful coexistence.

His explanations are what today we would call *evolutionary*. Nature has given us natural tendencies that somehow conspire to make these larger social institutions work for the general benefit. We may not understand how our private attempts to bargain, to communicate or to get along with others produce a general and beneficial system of economics, language or justice: but they do. Indeed, if they did not, and were destructive, society would not survive. What Smith is trying to work out is how these individual actions relate to the whole.

Smith on the philosophy of science

The History of Astronomy therefore has a deeper purpose than to tell the story of star-gazing – as its full title, *The Principles Which Lead and Direct Philosophical Enquiries; Illustrated by the History of Astronomy*, indicates. It is really about the human mind and how we analyse, categorise and understand the world. It starts by asking what leads us into scientific theorising, then shows how theories are proposed, tested and supplanted, and goes on to investigate what makes a 'good' theory, using the work of Isaac Newton as an example. It is all surprisingly modern, seeing science as an attempt to model the world – not about 'reality' but about human psychology and interpretation.

The distress of the unknown

Smith points out that we take familiar things for granted, without thinking. But when new things appear, it is a *surprise*.[1] It fills us with *wonder* about how they fit within our familiar world.[2] The feeling that something does not fit is uncomfortable; but our reason and imagination, and our capacities for abstraction and classification, help us to put the new phenomenon into context.

For example, we are surprised to see a piece of iron attracted by a magnet; but our imagination suggests that there is some force swirling around the stone, which helps us to explain the movement. It is a crude theory, but Smith wants to show how such theories are proposed, tested and improved on.

Conjectures and refutations

He does this by using the history of astronomy as an illustration.[3] For ancient astronomers the 'surprise' requiring explanation was the movement of the sun, moon and stars. One suggestion was that the sky was a dome-shaped roof, to which these bodies were attached and which moved daily from east to west. Unfortunately, that did not explain the erratic movement of the planets. So a more sophisticated theory was ventured: that there were in fact several spheres, one moving regularly east to west, and others

---

1   *The History of Astronomy*, section I.

2   Ibid., section II.

3   Ibid., section IV.

(bearing the planets) moving more erratically. But this erratic motion itself demanded some explanation. So more and more spheres were postulated, spinning one inside the other in different directions – until a total of 72 of them were imagined. The only trouble was that: 'This system had now become as intricate and complex as those appearances themselves, which it had been invented to render uniform and coherent.'[4]

Later astronomers looked for simpler explanations of the movements of the planets. Copernicus came up with a system that put the sun, not the earth, at the centre of the spheres. This made the erratic movement of the planets easier to explain, since in this interpretation the earth was also in motion. Although many people were shocked by the idea that the earth was not the hub of the universe, astronomers found it useful – at least until more accurate observations revealed its shortcomings.

But Isaac Newton was in turn able to come up with a simple, general explanation of not just how, but why, planets moved in exactly the way they were observed to. It was the effect of gravity. A few simple physical rules would explain the elliptical orbits of the planets and the appearance of other phenomena, such as comets, which could not be accommodated in the Copernican system. It seemed simple, almost graceful; and it fitted the observed facts.

Science and human understanding

To Smith, then, scientific method is a process of explaining the universe in ways that rest easily on the human mind; of reducing its complexities to simple principles that we can actually under-

---

4   Ibid., section IV, 8, p. 59.

stand. Models of the universe are proposed, tested, found wanting, modified and – when they become too cluttered or too much at odds with observation – are thrown out in favour of more elegant explanations. It is a remarkably modern view.

We see a certain beauty in theories that reduce a clutter of different observations into 'a few common principles'. That is because science is our own mental organisation. To Smith, all scientific models – 'all philosophical systems', in his words – 'are mere inventions of the imagination'.[5]

The psychology of communication

In the *Lectures on Rhetoric and Belles Lettres* too the heart of Smith's subject matter is in fact human psychology and the development, from that, of a key social institution – communication. For example, Smith advises, if you have a sympathetic audience, give them your whole message, then explain it bit by bit. If you face a hostile audience, do not assault them with your controversial conclusions all at once, but lead up to them in stages.

In the lectures – which exist only in the form of student notes – and in his essay *Considerations Concerning the First Formation of Languages*, Smith seeks to understand language by investigating how it emerged. Since there are no written records, Smith's history is necessarily conjectural; and his examples are limited to a few ancient and modern European languages. But his explanation is evolutionary: language grows, he believes, as human society develops, and is a tool of that development.

5   Ibid., section IV, 76, p. 105 (see also section II, 12, p. 46).

Communication and human nature

Because language is a product of the human mind, he asserts, it tells us something about our own nature. Take, for instance, our powers of categorisation, already observed in *The History of Astronomy*. Smith suggests that early peoples might have given different names to everything. That would become hugely cumbersome, but fortunately the human mind's power of abstraction comes to the rescue. We could see common characteristics in different things and so use a common word for whole classes of them – *trees*, for example. We can also define qualities such as colour – *the green tree* – or relations – *the tree above the cave*.[6] Such techniques, essential to scientific method, are no less valuable to our understanding of everyday life.

Smith's determination to apply forensic techniques to the subject unites all his enquiries, from *The Wealth of Nations* to the *Lectures on Rhetoric and Belles Lettres*. In the former, the quest is to identify the human motives driving production and exchange, and break them down into their component parts. In the latter, it is to discover the psychology behind communication and to analyse its structure and style.

The science of communication

Style, in fact, occupies much of Smith's attention. Good style, he insists, is concise, proper and precise.[7] It should convey the passion of the speaker or writer. It should be neat, clear and plain. Short

---

6   *Lectures on Rhetoric and Belles Lettres*, Lecture 3, v.19–v.24, pp. 10–11, and *Considerations Concerning the First Formation of Languages*, 12, p. 209.

7   *Lectures on Rhetoric and Belles Lettres*, Lecture 5, v.53, p. 23.

sentences help understanding.[8] And (a notion fundamental to *The Theory of Moral Sentiments*) language must evoke the empathy and acceptance of the listener.

Because communication is a matter of psychology, Smith insists that different arguments require different techniques. He goes through several – from *narrative* discourses that require an objective presentation, to *didactic* arguments that need to explain cause and effect, to various kinds of *oratorical* presentations that must reach the emotions. His illustrations show an extraordinary familiarity with the classical writers and historians.

The key, however, is that to communicate with people, you first have to understand them. Human beings are naturally very good at such empathy, which has allowed language to develop, from the earliest and crudest attempts to communicate, into a complex and highly beneficial social institution.

Smith on government and public policy

Smith's *Lectures on Jurisprudence* again survive only as the notes of his students.[9] By *jurisprudence*, they tell us, he means 'the theory of the general principles of law and government'[10] or 'the rules by which civil governments ought to be directed'.[11] Once again, the lectures can be seen as an exercise in social psychology, an attempt to trace how human interaction has caused us to build up bodies of law and government institutions.

The opening section is called *justice*, but covers a wide range

8   Ibid., Lecture 6.
9   *The Glasgow Edition* contains two versions, one a report of the 1762–3 session, and another dated 1766.
10 *Lectures on Jurisprudence*, Report dated 1766, p. 398.
11 Ibid., Report of 1762–3, Lecture of 24 December 1762.

of subjects, including the nature and development of government, constitutions, domestic law, slavery, property rights, courts and criminal justice. The other main section, on *police* (or policy), contains much of Smith's thinking on prices, money, trade and the division of labour that would shape his *The Wealth of Nations* more than a decade later.

Justice, government and law

Once again, Smith takes an evolutionary view. As hunter-gathering gave way to the age of nomadic shepherds, then to settled agriculture and to the age of commerce, different governmental and juridical systems were needed to underpin these economic arrangements. (A century later, Karl Marx would agree: the productive relations shape the social relations.[12])

Government, as Smith would elaborate in *The Wealth of Nations*, was created in order to defend property, which had become important in the ages of shepherds and farmers. The obvious utility of this arrangement was reinforced, he says, by our natural human tendency to respect authority. But it was the market economy which gave rise to democracy. Earlier, all power came from the local chief. In the exchange economy, producers had to direct more attention instead to the countless ordinary people who were their customers. Thus were sown the seeds of representative government.

---

12   Karl Marx, *The Poverty of Philosophy*, ch. 2, Second Observation.

Labour and exchange

Other passages also show that Smith was gestating *Wealth of Nations* even in the mid-1760s. 'It is the division of labour', he says, 'which increases the opulence of a country.' Here too is the example of the pin factory;[13] and the production of the woollen coat, which involves the collaboration of thousands of individuals and spreads employment through the society. And we are told that: 'When you apply to a brewer or butcher for beer or for beef you do not explain to him how much you stand in need of these, but how much it would be in [his] interest to allow you to have them for a certain price. You do not address his humanity, but his self love.'[14] (Perhaps the student simply failed to capture the poetry of Smith's original words.)

Similarly, we find Smith assaulting the mercantilist view that wealth is money and that imports must be restricted in order to conserve it. By riotous living, he points out, a rich prodigal can squander capital – which undermines output and prosperity, even though no coin has been lost from circulation. Wealth and money are clearly not the same thing.

As well as rehearsing *The Wealth of Nations*, the lectures develop the economic ideas in *The Theory of Moral Sentiments*. He insists that the driving force of our material progress is not our needs, but our wants, telling us that: 'Such is the delicacy of man alone that no object is produced to his liking.'[15] Economic progress does not grind to a halt once we are fed, clothed and housed. Our quest for improvement never ends and nor does

---

13 *Lectures on Jurisprudence*, Report of 1762–3, Lecture of 29 March 1763, pp. 341–2.

14 Ibid., Report of 1762–3, Lecture of 29 March 1763, p. 348.

15 Ibid., Report dated 1766, p. 487.

the progress in manufactures, industry, science and the arts that stems from it.

Incompetent government

If production, exchange and capital accumulation are the route to material progress, what blocks it? All too often, says Smith, it is incompetent government. Capital accumulation takes time. If people believe that the government cannot protect them against theft and leave them free to trade, they have little motive to be industrious and to save.

The *Lectures on Jurisprudence* were never intended for publication, and Smith's attack on government incompetence and interference is less inhibited than it is in *The Wealth of Nations*. But he has many of the same targets, including shortcomings in the law on contract, land tenure and the antiquated law of primogeniture; government subsidies, monopolies and privileges given to producers; and long apprenticeships, bondage and other regulations that prevent people from changing jobs.

Burdensome taxes are another roadblock. In the lectures, he has already started to think about the efficiency of taxes – preferring taxes on land to taxes on goods, because they are easier to collect. And there is, he thinks, far too much central planning from governments and from powerful landowners; people need markets and the freedom to trade, not direction from above.

Such interventions inevitably reduce public welfare. People enter into voluntary exchanges because both sides believe they will benefit. That is the source of human wealth. 'When two men trade between themselves,' he observes, 'it is undoubtedly for the advantage of both.' And, he tells the mercantilists: 'The case is exactly the same betwixt any two nations.'[16]

Freedom and progress

His policy prescriptions are equally robust:

> From the above considerations it appears that Britain should by all means be made a free port, that there should be no interruptions of any kind made to foreign trade, that if it were possible to defray the expenses of government by any other method, all duties, customs, and excise should be abolished, and that free commerce and liberty of exchange should be allowed with all nations and for all things.[17]

And, on the same reasoning, 'liberty of exchange' should be allowed for all things *within* all nations, too.

Some scholars of Smith's time presumed that progress was inevitable. After all, their world had certainly been progressing. Smith is not so sanguine. Progress requires a framework of rules, and security, and freedom, and justice. Otherwise, people lose their motivation to be industrious. Government undoubtedly has a role in maintaining all these. But it should also keep out of the way of the wealth-creating process and ensure that vested interests are not given the power to distort it. Once set free in this way, the natural desire of people to better their condition is a most powerful driver of progress.

---

16   Ibid., Report dated 1766, p. 511. He makes the same point at Report of 1762–3, Lecture of 13 April 1763, p. 390.

17   Ibid., Report dated 1766, p. 514.

Conclusion

Smith's less well-known writings may challenge the modern reader simply because of the depth of scholarship that they contain. In one, Smith talks knowledgeably and in depth about different historical cosmological models; in another, he is quoting references from various classical scholars to show how they used language; in another, he is comparing the legal institutions of a number of countries, both near and remote.

But as well as demonstrating Smith's mastery of a number of academic disciplines, they also show him clearly as a student of human nature. He does not hold that laws, governments, language or even science are simply 'given'. They are all, in fact, creations of the human mind. Yet they are complicated systems and not necessarily ones that we have consciously designed. What fascinates the scholar who speculates on the invisible hand is precisely how our individual actions conspire to produce those functioning social institutions.

6   A DIGRESSION ON THE INVISIBLE HAND

Adam Smith is famous for his 'invisible hand' idea. Most people take this to mean that our self-interested actions somehow produce an overall social benefit. Our hard bargaining, for example, creates a market system that allocates resources with great efficiency.

In fact, apart from a mention of the 'invisible hand of Jupiter' in *The History of Astronomy*, Smith uses the phrase just twice in his entire output and not really in the commonly presumed sense.

The rich make work for the poor

In *The Theory of Moral Sentiments*, Smith suggests that the hand of 'Providence' equalises economic rewards. The rich can eat no more than the poor. Their only use for most of the food produced by their land is to exchange it with others – those who supply the luxuries, the 'baubles and trinkets', that the rich demand. Thinking only of themselves, the rich provide employment to thousands:

> The rich only select from the heap what is most precious
> and agreeable. They consume little more than the poor,
> and in spite of their natural selfishness and rapacity,
> though they mean only their own conveniency, though
> the sole end which they propose from the labours of all
> the thousands whom they employ, be the gratification of

their own vain and insatiable desires, they divide with the poor the produce of all their improvements. They are led by an invisible hand to make nearly the same distribution of the necessaries of life, which would have been made, had the earth been divided into equal portions among all its inhabitants, and thus without intending it, without knowing it, advance the interest of the society, and afford means to the multiplication of the species.[1]

Domestic and foreign industry

The only mention of the invisible hand in *The Wealth of Nations* is in a passage about official monopolies that promote domestic industries over foreign trade. Smith notes that this induces people to commit more capital to home industries, and then slides into the point:

> As every individual ... endeavours as much as he can both to employ his capital in the support of domestic industry, and so to direct that industry that its produce may be of the greatest value; every individual necessarily labours to render the annual revenue of the society as great as he can. He generally, indeed, neither intends to promote the public interest, nor knows how much he is promoting it. By preferring the support of domestic to that of foreign industry, he intends only his own security; and by directing that industry in such a manner as its produce may be of the greatest value, he intends only his own gain, and he is in this, as in many other cases, led by an invisible hand to promote an end which was no part of his intention.[2]

---

1   *The Theory of Moral Sentiments*, part IV, ch. I, pp. 184–5, para. 10.
2   *The Wealth of Nations*, Book IV, ch. II, p. 456, para. 9.

These two passages suggest to critics that Adam Smith's real 'invisible hand' concept is far removed from the popular notion of it. In one, the happy outcome of self-interest is attributed to 'Providence'. In the other, it is a side comment in a discussion about the export trade.

Unintended consequences of human action

In fact, the critics read too narrowly. The invisible hand idea, as commonly understood, pervades Smith's work, and would do so even if these two specific references had never existed. For the phrase is a very convenient shorthand for Smith's idea that human actions have unintended consequences; and that provided a few fundamental rules such as the principles of justice are followed, the self-serving actions of individuals can unintentionally produce a well-functioning and beneficial overall social order.

When I buy a woollen coat (to use Smith's example),[3] I do it for my own benefit. I have scant regard for the welfare of the shopkeeper and even less for the weavers, shepherds, shearers, carders, dyers, spinners, toolmakers, carriers and all the rest – whom I will probably never even meet. Nor do any of them work on the coat in order to please me. Their thoughts are probably more about making money to feed their families.

And yet, my purchase does benefit them, because some small part of what I spend makes its way automatically to each of them. Likewise, the labour that each of them puts into the coat's manufacture gives me a better, cheaper garment than I could possibly make for myself.

---

3   Ibid., Book I, ch. I, p. 22, para. 11.

It may seem miraculous that the labour of thousands of people, in different countries, can be coordinated so automatically, without any need for a guiding authority, driven only by the self-interest of everyone involved. But Smith explains it quite simply. Voluntary exchange happens only when both sides expect to benefit from the bargain. They each get something they want in return for something they do not want so much – money in return for labour, say, or goods in return for money. When millions of people trade with each other in this way, such benefit spreads widely and rapidly through the whole community.

Prices, meanwhile, show how much people are willing to sacrifice to get particular goods and services in exchange. They signal to us where our labour and capital should be steered in order to reap the highest returns. And thus – automatically but quite unintentionally – we end up satisfying the community's most important wants and needs.

A self-perpetuating system

Smith seems to have some inkling of the evolutionary nature of this social system. It survives, he says, because it works. In *The Theory of Moral Sentiments*, true enough, he attributes it to divine or semi-divine providence. Since academic life was then ruled by clerics, perhaps he had no choice. Or perhaps, a century before Darwin, it seemed the only explanation. Yet he wavers between ascribing the system to the deity and to nature; and later, when free of the clerics and on an independent salary, the idea that this is a natural, self-perpetuating system seems to grow stronger in his thoughts.[4]

---

4   I am grateful to Professor Gavin Kennedy for this observation.

That is not to say that we can simply do as we please and the invisible hand will take care of us. Smith is well aware that human beings can be self-centred, envious, vain and resentful. In excess, these natural human tendencies are destructive; though in moderation, they are crucially important. Our self-interest drives us to make bargains, unintentionally benefiting others. Our envy of the rich inspires us to great efforts, which happen to advance manufacture, science, even the arts. Because we love the esteem of others, our vanity prompts us into acts of benevolence. Since others' resentment distresses us, we avoid doing them injury.

In an odd way, therefore, Adam Smith's moral system is as self-centred as his economic system. We benefit others as a by-product of our own ambition, and avoid harming them in order to avoid the distress of their contempt.

Individual action and social outcomes

But for this social system to function smoothly and automatically, we have to follow some rules: the rules of justice, which prevent us harming others; the rules of morality, which urge us to curb our raw desires; and, in the economic sphere, rules of property and contract. These rules of individual behaviour conspire to create a beneficial social order. We may not understand how: but our natural instinct is in any case a surer guide than our limited reason and understanding.

More recently, the Nobel economist F. A. Hayek traced the idea that harmonious social orders could arise without the need for central commands back to Smith and beyond.[5] With

---

5   See F. A. Hayek, *Studies in Philosophy, Politics and Economics*, Simon & Schuster, New York, 1967, ch. 6, 'The results of human action but not of human design',

his modern understanding of evolution and psychology, Hayek worked out how social groups could prosper, and unwittingly create a smoothly functioning order, simply by following certain regularities of individual behaviour.[6] In language, for example, we unintentionally create a hugely effective communication system simply by following a few rules of grammar – rules that we follow quite naturally, but find hard to explain. Smith, of course, gets close to that in his own remarks on language.[7]

The foundation of this beneficial social order lies in our learning to live together. We all want to satisfy our own desires, but often these are in conflict with the desires of others. Gradually we learn what actions are tolerated by others and do not lead to a destructive violence. And so, helped by a natural human empathy, we work out the rules of justice, by which we can pursue our own interests without harming others.[8] Not only in the economic sphere, but in other social interaction too, we learn to collaborate in ways that benefit us all, even though that may not be any part of our intention.

---

pp. 96–105. For a readable overview, see E. Butler, *Hayek: His Contribution to the Political and Economic Thought of Our Time*, Temple Smith, London, 1983, ch. 1, 'Understanding how society works'.

6   Hayek, *Studies in Philosophy*, ch. 4, 'Notes on the evolution of rules of conduct', pp. 66–81.

7   See *Lectures on Rhetoric and Belles Lettres*.

8   *The Theory of Moral Sentiments*, part II, section II, ch. III.

7   SOME OF ADAM SMITH'S FAMOUS QUOTATIONS

For a wider selection of quotations from Adam Smith, see J. Haggarty, *The Wisdom of Adam Smith*, Liberty Fund, Indianapolis, IN, 1976.

On the division of labour ...

It is the great multiplication of the productions of all the different arts, in consequence of the division of labour, which occasions, in a well-governed society, that universal opulence which extends itself to the lowest ranks of the people.

The Wealth of Nations, Book I, ch. I, p. 22, para. 10

... and comparative advantage

By means of glasses, hotbeds, and hotwalls, very good grapes can be raised in Scotland, and very good wine too can be made of them at about thirty times the expense for which at least equally good can be brought from foreign countries. Would it be a reasonable law to prohibit the importation of all foreign wines, merely to encourage the making of claret and burgundy in Scotland?

The Wealth of Nations, Book IV, ch. II, p. 458, para. 15

It is the maxim of every prudent master of a family, never to attempt to make at home what it will cost him more to make than to buy … What is prudence in the conduct of every private family, can scarce be folly in that of a great kingdom.

The Wealth of Nations, Book IV, ch. II, pp. 456–7, paras 11–12

On competition …

In general, if any branch of trade, or any division of labour, be advantageous to the public, the freer and more general the competition, it will always be the more so.

The Wealth of Nations, Book II, ch. II, p. 329, para. 106

Consumption is the sole end and purpose of all production; and the interest of the producer ought to be attended to, only so far as it may be necessary for promoting that of the consumer.

The Wealth of Nations, Book IV, ch. VIII, p. 660, para. 49

… and the distortion of trade

People of the same trade seldom meet together, even for merriment and diversion, but the conversation ends in a conspiracy against the public, or in some contrivance to raise prices. … But though the law cannot hinder people of the same trade from sometimes assembling together, it ought to do nothing to facilitate such assemblies, much less to render them necessary.

The Wealth of Nations, Book IV, ch. VIII, p. 145, para. c27

A regulation which obliges all those of the same trade in a particular town to enter their names and places of abode in a public register, facilitates such assemblies ...

A regulation which enables those of the same trade to tax themselves in order to provide for their poor, their sick, their widows and orphans ... renders such assemblies necessary.

An incorporation not only renders them necessary, but makes the act of the majority binding upon the whole. In a free trade, an effectual combination cannot be established but by the unanimous consent of every single trader, and it cannot last longer than every single trader continues of the same mind. The majority of a corporation can enact a bye-law, with proper penalties, which will limit the competition more effectually and more durably than any voluntary combination whatever.

   The Wealth of Nations, Book IV, ch. VIII, p. 145, paras c29–30

To widen the market and to narrow the competition, is always the interest of the dealers ... The proposal of any new law or regulation of commerce which comes from this order, ought always to be listened to with great precaution, and ought never to be adopted till after having been long and carefully examined, not only with the most scrupulous, but with the most suspicious attention. It comes from an order of men, whose interest is never exactly the same with that of the public, who have generally an interest to deceive and even oppress the public, and who accordingly have, upon many occasions, both deceived and oppressed it.

   The Wealth of Nations, Book I, ch. XI, p. 267, para. 10

On government ...

It is the highest impertinence and presumption ... in kings and ministers, to pretend to watch over the economy of private people, and to restrain their expense ... They are themselves always, and without any exception, the greatest spendthrifts in the society. Let them look well after their own expense, and they may safely trust private people with theirs. If their own extravagance does not ruin the state, that of their subjects never will.

> *The Wealth of Nations*, Book II, ch. III, p. 346, para. 36

The statesman who should attempt to direct private people in what manner they ought to employ their capitals, would not only load himself with a most unnecessary attention, but assume an authority which could safely be trusted, not only to no single person, but to no council or senate whatever, and which would nowhere be so dangerous as in the hands of a man who had folly and presumption enough to fancy himself fit to exercise it.

> *The Wealth of Nations*, Book IV, ch. II, p. 456, para. 10

... taxation ...

There is no art which one government sooner learns of another than that of draining money from the pockets of the people.

> *The Wealth of Nations*, Book V, ch. II, part II, Appendix to articles I & II, p. 861, para. 12

The subjects of every state ought to contribute towards the support of the government, as nearly as possible, in proportion to their respective abilities ...

> *The Wealth of Nations*, Book V, ch. II, part II, v.ii, p. 825, para. 3

The tax which each individual is bound to pay ought to be certain, and not arbitrary. The time of payment, the manner of payment, the quantity to be paid, ought all to be clear and plain to the contributor, and to every other person ...
> *The Wealth of Nations*, Book V, ch. II, part II, p. 825, para. 4

Every tax ought to be levied at the time, or in the manner, in which it is most likely to be convenient for the contributor to pay ...
> *The Wealth of Nations*, Book V, ch. II, part II, p. 826, para. 5

Every tax ought to be so contrived as both to take out and to keep out of the pockets of the people as little as possible, over and above what it brings into the public treasury of the state ...
> *The Wealth of Nations*, Book V, ch. II, part II, p. 826, para. 6

The proprietor of stock is necessarily a citizen of the world, and is not necessarily attached to any particular country. He would be apt to abandon the country in which he was exposed to a vexatious inquisition, in order to be assessed to a burdensome tax, and would remove his stock to some other country where he could either carry on his business, or enjoy his fortune more at his ease.
> *Wealth of Nations*, Book V, ch. II, article II, pp. 848–9, para. f8

... and subsidies

The bounty to the white-herring fishery is a tonnage bounty; and is proportioned to the burden of the ship, not to her diligence or success in the fishery; and it has, I am afraid, been too common for vessels to fit out for the sole purpose of catching, not the fish, but the bounty.

The Wealth of Nations, Book IV, ch. V, p. 520, para. 32

On import controls

As a rich man is likely to be a better customer to the industrious people in his neighbourhood than a poor, so is likewise a rich nation. [Trade restrictions,] by aiming at the impoverishment of all our neighbours, tend to render that very commerce insignificant and contemptible.

The Wealth of Nations, Book IV, ch. III, part II, p. 495, para. c11

To judge whether such retaliations [tariffs imposed against other high-tariff countries] are likely to produce such an effect does not, perhaps, belong so much to the science of a legislator, whose deliberations ought to be governed by general principles which are always the same, as to the skill of that insidious and crafty animal, vulgarly called a statesman or politician, whose councils are directed by the momentary fluctuations of affairs.

The Wealth of Nations, Book IV, ch. II, p. 468, para. 39

On incentives …

Public services are never better performed than when their reward comes in consequence of their being performed, and is proportioned to the diligence employed in performing them.

The Wealth of Nations, Book V, ch. I, part II, p. 719, para. b20

... and perverse incentives

It is the interest of every man to live as much at his ease as he can; and if his emoluments are to be precisely the same, whether he does, or does not perform some very laborious duty, it is certainly his interest ... either to neglect it altogether, or ... to perform it in [a] careless and slovenly manner.

The Wealth of Nations, Book V, ch. I, part III, article II, p. 760, para. f7

On justice ...

If [justice] is removed, the great, the immense fabric of human society ... must in a moment crumble into atoms.

The Theory of Moral Sentiments, part II, section II, ch. III, p. 86, para. 4

Little else is requisite to carry a state to the highest degree of opulence from the lowest barbarism, but peace, easy taxes, and a tolerable administration of justice: all the rest being brought about by the natural course of things.

Lecture in 1755, quoted in Dugald Stewart, *Account of the life and writings of Adam Smith LLD*, section IV, 25

... and human empathy

How selfish soever man may be supposed, there are evidently some principles in his nature, which interest him in the fortune of others, and render their happiness necessary to him, though he derives nothing from it, except the pleasure of seeing it.

The Theory of Moral Sentiments, part I, section I, ch. I, p. 9, para. 1

On the drive to improve ...

The natural effort of every individual to better his own condition ... is so powerful, that it is alone, and without any assistance, not only capable of carrying on the society to wealth and prosperity, but of surmounting a hundred impertinent obstructions with which the folly of human laws too often encumbers its operations.

The Wealth of Nations, Book IV, ch. V, Digression on the Corn Trade, p. 540, para. b43

... the invisible hand ...

[The rich] consume little more than the poor, and in spite of their natural selfishness and rapacity ... they divide with the poor the produce of all their improvements. They are led by an invisible hand to make nearly the same distribution of the necessaries of life, which would have been made, had the earth been divided into equal portions among all its inhabitants, and thus without intending it, without knowing it, advance the interest of the society, and afford means to the multiplication of the species.

The Theory of Moral Sentiments, part IV, ch. I, pp. 184–5, para. 10

Every individual ... neither intends to promote the public interest, nor knows how much he is promoting it ... he intends only his own security; and by directing that industry in such a manner as its produce may be of the greatest value, he intends only his own gain, and he is in this, as in many other cases, led by an invisible hand to promote an end which was no part of his intention.

The Wealth of Nations, Book IV, ch. II, p. 456, para. 9

It is not from the benevolence of the butcher, the brewer, or the baker, that we expect our dinner, but from their regard to their own interest. We address ourselves, not to their humanity but to their self-love, and never talk to them of our necessities but of their advantages.

> *The Wealth of Nations*, Book I, ch. II, pp. 26–7, para. 12

... and planning

The man of system ... is apt to be very wise in his own conceit; and is often so enamoured with the supposed beauty of his own ideal plan of government, that he cannot suffer the smallest deviation from any part of it ... He seems to imagine that he can arrange the different members of a great society with as much ease as the hand arranges the different pieces upon a chess-board. He does not consider that in the great chess-board of human society, every single piece has a principle of motion of its own, altogether different from that which the legislature might choose to impress upon it.

> *The Theory of Moral Sentiments*, part VI, section II, ch. II, pp. 233–4, para. 17

On universities

In the university of Oxford, the greater part of the public professors have, for these many years, given up altogether even the pretence of teaching.

> *The Wealth of Nations*, Book V, ch. I, part III, article II, p. 761, para. 8

The discipline of colleges and universities is in general contrived, not for the benefit of the students, but for the interest, or more properly speaking, for the ease of the masters.

The Wealth of Nations, Book V, ch. I, part III, article II, p. 764, para. 15

On the distribution of wealth ...

What improves the circumstances of the greater part can never be regarded as an inconveniency to the whole. No society can surely be flourishing and happy, of which the far greater part of the members are poor and miserable.

The Wealth of Nations, Book I, ch. VIII, p. 96, para. 36

No complaint, however, is more common than that of a scarcity of money.

The Wealth of Nations, Book IV, ch. I, p. 437, para. 16

... and the benefits of freedom

[Without trade restrictions] the obvious and simple system of natural liberty establishes itself of its own accord. Every man ... is left perfectly free to pursue his own interest in his own way. ... The sovereign is completely discharged from a duty [for which] no human wisdom or knowledge could ever be sufficient; the duty of superintending the industry of private people, and of directing it towards the employments most suitable to the interest of the society.

The Wealth of Nations, Book IV, ch. IX, p. 687, para. 51

8 SELECT BIBLIOGRAPHY

The Glasgow Edition of the Works and Correspondence of Adam Smith

Bryce, J. C. (ed.) (1985), *Lectures on Rhetoric and Belle Lettres*, Indianapolis, IN: Liberty Fund.

Campbell, R. H., and A. S. Skinner (eds) (1982), *An Inquiry into the Nature and Causes of the Wealth of Nations*, Indianapolis, IN: Liberty Fund.

Haakonssen, K., and A. S. Skinner (2003), *Index to the Works of Adam Smith*, Indianapolis, IN: Liberty Fund.

Meek, R. I., D. D. Raphael and P. G. Stein (eds) (1982), *Lectures on Jurisprudence*, Indianapolis, IN: Liberty Fund.

Mossner, E. C., and I. S. Ross (eds) (1987), *Correspondence of Adam Smith*, revised edn, Indianapolis, IN: Liberty Fund.

Raphael, D. D., and A. L. Macfie (eds) (1984), *The Theory of Moral Sentiments*, Indianapolis, IN: Liberty Fund.

Wightman, W. P. D., and J. C. Bryce (eds) (1982), *Essays on Philosophical Subjects*, Indianapolis, IN: Liberty Fund (this volume includes Dugald Stewart's 'Account of the life and writings of Adam Smith LLD').

Other editions of Smith's works

Haggarty, J. (1976), *The Wisdom of Adam Smith*, Indianapolis, IN: Liberty Fund (collection of key quotations from Smith's works).

Heilbroner, R. L., with L. J. Malone (1986), *The Essential Adam Smith*, Oxford: Oxford University Press (abridged version of Smith's main writing, with introductory notes).

Books about Smith and his work

Buchan, J. (2006), *Adam Smith and the Pursuit of Perfect Liberty*, London: Profile Books (arguing that Smith's ideas do not fit within modern political categories).

Campbell, R. H., and A. S. Skinner (1982), *Adam Smith*, London: Croome Helm (biography with clear summaries of Smith's main works).

Fry, M. (ed.) (1992), *Adam Smith's Legacy*, London: Routledge (Smith's place in modern economics, as seen by Paul Samuelson, Franco Modigliani, James Buchanan and other prominent economists).

Kennedy, G. (2005), *Adam Smith's Lost Legacy*, London: Palgrave Macmillan (focusing on Smith's moral philosophy, Kennedy argues that Smith is often misinterpreted today).

McLean, I. (2006), *Adam Smith: Radical and Egalitarian*, Edinburgh: Edinburgh University Press (the title says it all).

O'Rourke, P. J. (2006), *On The Wealth of Nations*, New York: Atlantic Monthly Press (witty but perceptive summary of Smith's main ideas). ·

Rae, J. (1895), *Life of Adam Smith*, London: Macmillan (engaging biography, also reprinted in 1965 with an introduction by Jacob Viner).

Ross, I. S. (1995), *The Life of Adam Smith*, Oxford: Oxford University Press (full-scale biography by a leading Smith scholar).

West, E. G. (1976), *Adam Smith: The Man and His Works*, Indianapolis, IN: Liberty Fund (excellent overview of Smith's life and contribution).

Articles on Smith and his work

Rosten, L. (1970), 'A modest man named Smith', in *People I Have Loved, Known, or Admired*, New York: McGraw-Hill.

Sprague, E. (1967), 'Adam Smith', in P. Edwards (ed.), *The Encyclopaedia of Philosophy*, London and New York: Collier Macmillan (straightforward and concise exposition, concentrating on Smith's moral philosophy).

DVD

Adam Smith and the Wealth of Nations, Indianapolis, IN: Liberty Fund.

COMMENTARY: THE RELEVANCE OF ADAM SMITH TODAY
Craig Smith[1]

To most people, particularly in his homeland of Scotland, Adam Smith is a famous figure. A statue is being raised in his honour in Edinburgh, banknotes bear his likeness and a college and a theatre are named after him. I even write this from my office in the Adam Smith Building at the University of Glasgow. Sadly, however, Smith is known and celebrated without enough people knowing and celebrating what he actually thought. Smith was one of the most profound thinkers to emerge from Scotland, Britain and indeed Europe. Hopefully this Adam Smith primer will go some way towards correcting this widespread public ignorance.

My first contact with Adam Smith came through an enlightened high school economics teacher who used examples from *The Wealth of Nations* to enliven lessons. Fourth period on a Wednesday was an intellectual delight filled with pin-makers, working men's woollen coats and butchers, brewers and bakers. I was fortunate to have such an early experience of the great man's work and even more fortunate to be able to take a class on the Scottish Enlightenment as part of my undergraduate studies.

Unfortunately the early experience of Smith's thought that I

---

1   At the time of writing Craig Smith was British Academy Postdoctoral Fellow in the Department of Politics at the University of Glasgow. By the time of publication he will be lecturer in the Department of Moral Philosophy at the University of St Andrews.

enjoyed is all too rare. Today not enough students and lay people have read Smith's work. Smith is not taught as often as he ought to be in our schools and universities. This is a great shame. It is particularly unfortunate that many undergraduate economics students are given only a cursory introduction to the founding father of their discipline. Many economics courses mention Smith (and usually the pin-making example) only briefly in the introductory lectures on the division of labour before passing on to discuss the very principles he identified in dry abstract terms.

This is a pity, because Smith writes in a clear manner that is as accessible today as it was 250 years ago. His writings are a rich and complex body of observations that can inspire and enlighten. Smith's work represents an attempt to understand how complex societies actually work. This social science has at its heart an awareness of the crucial reality of individual interaction and interdependence. Both of these are realities of the world in which we live today.

In a world of globalisation Smith's study of international and domestic trade cuts straight to the heart of the forces that shape all our lives. He may have been writing in a different age but his diagnosis of the errors of mercantilism and his general distrust of arbitrary political interference are particularly relevant today in a world where commerce is easily demonised by those opposed to the supposed effects of trade.

Smith has his fair share of opponents among intellectuals. But the Smith that they dismiss as the prophet of selfishness is not a Smith that would be recognised by anyone who had actually read and understood his work. *The Theory of Moral Sentiments* is a deeply humane work of moral psychology that rightly places empathy at the heart of human experience. Smith spent his adult life studying and explaining everyday human experience. He was not obsessed by unattainable ideas of perfect virtue. Instead he spent his time examining how normal people actually experience social interaction and how they go about making moral decisions.

Nor is there, as some superficial critics suggest, a contradiction between the study of trade in *The Wealth of Nations* and the analysis of sympathy in *The Theory of Moral Sentiments*. Both are facets of the human experience and Smith deploys the same conceptual rigour in examining the implications of both for human social life.

Smith's work is grounded in a desire to understand the empirical reality of human social life. For example, his arguments against excessive political interference are based on a factual analysis of the reality of commercial exchange. It is also too often overlooked that his examples of the productive benefits of exchange between individuals are not the very wealthy – whom he often disdains – but the very poor. Smith believed that trade benefits everyone and in particular those at the very bottom of society.

Adam Smith's work provides a clear analysis of the fundamental principles and institutions necessary to support a free society. The rule of law and justice provide the framework for the 'simple and obvious' system of natural liberty that benefits all of mankind. While the evolution of shared moral practices supports and sustains human community life.

It is the idea of the invisible hand, or more generally the idea of social evolution through unintended consequences, which represents Smith's chief legacy to the modern world. The recognition that many of the most important human achievements are, as Smith's friend Adam Ferguson observed, the results of human action, not the product of human design, is a profound lesson to us all. It is this observation which leads Smith to his deep scepticism towards 'men of system' who would organise humanity to achieve noble ends.

Smith was a practical, circumspect man and his thought does not lend itself easily to the hubris of the political ideologue. This is not to say that Smith should not be considered as a radical thinker. For his own time his ideas were revolutionary. In our time his ideas point towards a political outlook that is best characterised as humane and liberal. They remain radical because they challenge many of the settled assumptions of our political class. Perhaps if more of our politicians had read and understood Smith's work what appears radical would be recognised as the commonsense, fact-based advice it truly is.

There can be little doubt that, in academia, Adam Smith scholarship is in a healthy state. Between 2000 and 2004 more than fourteen graduate students from around the world completed PhDs on Adam Smith. They join an international community of Adam Smith scholars that operates across the academic disciplines. The publication of an annual *Adam Smith Review* by the International Adam Smith Society is further testament to the vigour of the academic interest in Smith's work.

Aside from scholars of Adam Smith there is also a healthy community of scholars inspired by Smith. There is ample room for those inspired by his observations to extend them through their own work. Interest in Smith's 'remarkably modern' theory of science is growing and his social psychology of morality is encouraging research in the new sub-discipline of evolutionary psychology. His theories of language and aesthetics remain underexplored and offer more fertile ground to scholars. As Dr Butler's primer ably indicates, Smith left a broad intellectual legacy. But he also left an unfinished legacy. Exploring the implications of Smith's thought provides a rich and exciting research project that could last a lifetime.

Adam Smith has left us an amazingly rich legacy of writing. He is a figure who has helped to shape the world in which we live today. He is also a figure who provides us with the intellectual toolkit to understand that world. His work should be more widely read and more clearly understood. If this were the case then the inspirational power of his ideas would help to enlighten our own world, just as his insights helped to enlighten his own time.

ABOUT THE IEA

The Institute is a research and educational charity (No. CC 235 351), limited by guarantee. Its mission is to improve understanding of the fundamental institutions of a free society by analysing and expounding the role of markets in solving economic and social problems.

The IEA achieves its mission by:

- a high-quality publishing programme
- conferences, seminars, lectures and other events
- outreach to school and college students
- brokering media introductions and appearances

The IEA, which was established in 1955 by the late Sir Antony Fisher, is an educational charity, not a political organisation. It is independent of any political party or group and does not carry on activities intended to affect support for any political party or candidate in any election or referendum, or at any other time. It is financed by sales of publications, conference fees and voluntary donations.

In addition to its main series of publications the IEA also publishes a quarterly journal, *Economic Affairs*.

The IEA is aided in its work by a distinguished international Academic Advisory Council and an eminent panel of Honorary Fellows. Together with other academics, they review prospective IEA publications, their comments being passed on anonymously to authors. All IEA papers are therefore subject to the same rigorous independent refereeing process as used by leading academic journals.

IEA publications enjoy widespread classroom use and course adoptions in schools and universities. They are also sold throughout the world and often translated/reprinted.

Since 1974 the IEA has helped to create a worldwide network of 100 similar institutions in over 70 countries. They are all independent but share the IEA's mission.

Views expressed in the IEA's publications are those of the authors, not those of the Institute (which has no corporate view), its Managing Trustees, Academic Advisory Council members or senior staff.

Members of the Institute's Academic Advisory Council, Honorary Fellows, Trustees and Staff are listed on the following page.

The Institute gratefully acknowledges financial support for its publications programme and other work from a generous benefaction by the late Alec and Beryl Warren.

125

Other papers recently published by the IEA include:

WHO, What and Why?
Transnational Government, Legitimacy and the World Health Organization
Roger Scruton
Occasional Paper 113; ISBN 0 255 36487 3; £8.00

The World Turned Rightside Up
A New Trading Agenda for the Age of Globalisation
John C. Hulsman
Occasional Paper 114; ISBN 0 255 36495 4; £8.00

The Representation of Business in English Literature
Introduced and edited by Arthur Pollard
Readings 53; ISBN 0 255 36491 1; £12.00

Anti-Liberalism 2000
The Rise of New Millennium Collectivism
David Henderson
Occasional Paper 115; ISBN 0 255 36497 0; £7.50

Capitalism, Morality and Markets
Brian Griffiths, Robert A. Sirico, Norman Barry & Frank Field
Readings 54; ISBN 0 255 36496 2; £7.50

A Conversation with Harris and Seldon
Ralph Harris & Arthur Seldon
Occasional Paper 116; ISBN 0 255 36498 9; £7.50

Malaria and the DDT Story
Richard Tren & Roger Bate
Occasional Paper 117; ISBN 0 255 36499 7; £10.00

A Plea to Economists Who Favour Liberty: Assist the Everyman
Daniel B. Klein
Occasional Paper 118; ISBN 0 255 36501 2; £10.00

The Changing Fortunes of Economic Liberalism
Yesterday, Today and Tomorrow
David Henderson
Occasional Paper 105 (new edition); ISBN 0 255 36520 9; £12.50

The Global Education Industry
Lessons from Private Education in Developing Countries
James Tooley
Hobart Paper 141 (new edition); ISBN 0 255 36503 9; £12.50

Saving Our Streams
The Role of the Anglers' Conservation Association in
Protecting English and Welsh Rivers
Roger Bate
Research Monograph 53; ISBN 0 255 36494 6; £10.00

Better Off Out?
The Benefits or Costs of EU Membership
Brian Hindley & Martin Howe
Occasional Paper 99 (new edition); ISBN 0 255 36502 0; £10.00

Buckingham at 25
Freeing the Universities from State Control
Edited by James Tooley
Readings 55; ISBN 0 255 36512 8; £15.00

Lectures on Regulatory and Competition Policy
Irwin M. Stelzer
Occasional Paper 120; ISBN 0 255 36511 X; ,12.50

Misguided Virtue
False Notions of Corporate Social Responsibility
David Henderson
Hobart Paper 142; ISBN 0 255 36510 1; £12.50

HIV and Aids in Schools
The Political Economy of Pressure Groups and Miseducation
Barrie Craven, Pauline Dixon, Gordon Stewart & James Tooley
Occasional Paper 121; ISBN 0 255 36522 5; £10.00

The Road to Serfdom
The Reader's Digest *condensed version*
Friedrich A. Hayek
Occasional Paper 122; ISBN 0 255 36530 6; £7.50

Bastiat's *The Law*
Introduction by Norman Barry
Occasional Paper 123; ISBN 0 255 36509 8; £7.50

A Globalist Manifesto for Public Policy
Charles Calomiris
Occasional Paper 124; ISBN 0 255 36525 x; £7.50

Euthanasia for Death Duties
Putting Inheritance Tax Out of Its Misery
Barry Bracewell-Milnes
Research Monograph 54; ISBN 0 255 36513 6; £10.00

Liberating the Land
The Case for Private Land-use Planning
Mark Pennington
Hobart Paper 143; ISBN 0 255 36508 x; £10.00

IEA Yearbook of Government Performance 2002/2003
Edited by Peter Warburton
Yearbook 1; ISBN 0 255 36532 2; £15.00

Britain's Relative Economic Performance, 1870–1999
Nicholas Crafts
Research Monograph 55; ISBN 0 255 36524 1; £10.00

Should We Have Faith in Central Banks?
Otmar Issing
Occasional Paper 125; ISBN 0 255 36528 4; £7.50

The Dilemma of Democracy
Arthur Seldon
Hobart Paper 136 (reissue); ISBN 0 255 36536 5; £10.00

Capital Controls: a 'Cure' Worse Than the Problem?
Forrest Capie
Research Monograph 56; ISBN 0 255 36506 3; £10.00

The Poverty of 'Development Economics'
Deepak Lal
Hobart Paper 144 (reissue); ISBN 0 255 36519 5; £15.00

Should Britain Join the Euro?
The Chancellor's Five Tests Examined
Patrick Minford
Occasional Paper 126; ISBN 0 255 36527 6; £7.50

Post-Communist Transition: Some Lessons
Leszek Balcerowicz
Occasional Paper 127; ISBN 0 255 36533 0; £7.50

A Tribute to Peter Bauer
John Blundell et al.
Occasional Paper 128; ISBN 0 255 36531 4; £10.00

Employment Tribunals
Their Growth and the Case for Radical Reform
J. R. Shackleton
Hobart Paper 145; ISBN 0 255 36515 2; £10.00

Fifty Economic Fallacies Exposed
Geoffrey E. Wood
Occasional Paper 129; ISBN 0 255 36518 7; £12.50

A Market in Airport Slots

Keith Boyfield (editor), David Starkie, Tom Bass & Barry Humphreys
Readings 56; ISBN 0 255 36505 5; £10.00

Money, Inflation and the Constitutional Position of the Central Bank

Milton Friedman & Charles A. E. Goodhart
Readings 57; ISBN 0 255 36538 1; £10.00

railway.com

Parallels between the Early British Railways and the ICT Revolution
Robert C. B. Miller
Research Monograph 57; ISBN 0 255 36534 9; £12.50

The Regulation of Financial Markets

Edited by Philip Booth & David Currie
Readings 58; ISBN 0 255 36551 9; £12.50

Climate Alarmism Reconsidered

Robert L. Bradley Jr
Hobart Paper 146; ISBN 0 255 36541 1; £12.50

Government Failure: E. G. West on Education

Edited by James Tooley & James Stanfield
Occasional Paper 130; ISBN 0 255 36552 7; £12.50

Corporate Governance: Accountability in the Marketplace

Elaine Sternberg
Second edition
Hobart Paper 147; ISBN 0 255 36542 x; £12.50

The Land Use Planning System

Evaluating Options for Reform
John Corkindale
Hobart Paper 148; ISBN 0 255 36550 0; £10.00

Economy and Virtue
Essays on the Theme of Markets and Morality
Edited by Dennis O'Keeffe
Readings 59; ISBN 0 255 36504 7; £12.50

Free Markets Under Siege
Cartels, Politics and Social Welfare
Richard A. Epstein
Occasional Paper 132; ISBN 0 255 36553 5; £10.00

Unshackling Accountants
D. R. Myddelton
Hobart Paper 149; ISBN 0 255 36559 4; £12.50

The Euro as Politics
Pedro Schwartz
Research Monograph 58; ISBN 0 255 36535 7; £12.50

Pricing Our Roads
Vision and Reality
Stephen Glaister & Daniel J. Graham
Research Monograph 59; ISBN 0 255 36562 4; £10.00

The Role of Business in the Modern World
Progress, Pressures, and Prospects for the Market Economy
David Henderson
Hobart Paper 150; ISBN 0 255 36548 9; £12.50

Public Service Broadcasting Without the BBC?
Alan Peacock
Occasional Paper 133; ISBN 0 255 36565 9; £10.00

The ECB and the Euro: the First Five Years
Otmar Issing
Occasional Paper 134; ISBN 0 255 36555 1; £10.00

Towards a Liberal Utopia?
Edited by Philip Booth
Hobart Paperback 32; ISBN 0 255 36563 2; £15.00

The Way Out of the Pensions Quagmire
Philip Booth & Deborah Cooper
Research Monograph 60; ISBN 0 255 36517 9; £12.50

Black Wednesday
A Re-examination of Britain's Experience in the Exchange Rate Mechanism
Alan Budd
Occasional Paper 135; ISBN 0 255 36566 7; £7.50

Crime: Economic Incentives and Social Networks
Paul Ormerod
Hobart Paper 151; ISBN 0 255 36554 3; £10.00

The Road to Serfdom *with* **The Intellectuals and Socialism**
Friedrich A. Hayek
Occasional Paper 136; ISBN 0 255 36576 4; £10.00

Money and Asset Prices in Boom and Bust
Tim Congdon
Hobart Paper 152; ISBN 0 255 36570 5; £10.00

The Dangers of Bus Re-regulation
and Other Perspectives on Markets in Transport
John Hibbs et al.
Occasional Paper 137; ISBN 0 255 36572 1; £10.00

The New Rural Economy
Change, Dynamism and Government Policy
Berkeley Hill et al.
Occasional Paper 138; ISBN 0 255 36546 2; £15.00

The Benefits of Tax Competition
Richard Teather
Hobart Paper 153; ISBN 0 255 36569 1; £12.50

Wheels of Fortune
Self-funding Infrastructure and the Free Market Case for a Land Tax
Fred Harrison
Hobart Paper 154; ISBN 0 255 36589 6; £12.50

Were 364 Economists All Wrong?
Edited by Philip Booth
Readings 60
ISBN-13: 978 0 255 36588 8; £10.00

Europe After the 'No' Votes
Mapping a New Economic Path
Patrick A. Messerlin
Occasional Paper 139
ISBN-13: 978 0 255 36580 2; £10.00

The Railways, the Market and the Government
John Hibbs et al.
Readings 61
ISBN-13: 978 0 255 36567 3; £12.50

Corruption: The World's Big C
Cases, Causes, Consequences, Cures
Ian Senior
Research Monograph 61
ISBN-13: 978 0 255 36571 0; £12.50

Choice and the End of Social Housing
Peter King
Hobart Paper 155
ISBN-13: 978 0 255 36568 0; £10.00

Sir Humphrey's Legacy
Facing Up to the Cost of Public Sector Pensions
Neil Record
Hobart Paper 156
ISBN-13: 978 0 255 36578 9; £10.00

The Economics of Law
Cento Veljanovski
Second edition
Hobart Paper 157
ISBN-13: 978 0 255 36561 1; £12.50

Living with Leviathan
Public Spending, Taxes and Economic Performance
David B. Smith
Hobart Paper 158
ISBN-13: 978 0 255 36579 6; £12.50

The Vote Motive
Gordon Tullock
New edition
Hobart Paperback 33
ISBN-13: 978 0 255 36577 2; £10.00

Waging the War of Ideas
John Blundell
Third edition
Occasional Paper 131
ISBN-13: 978 0 255 36606 9; £12.50

The War Between the State and the Family
How Government Divides and Impoverishes
Patricia Morgan
Hobart Paper 159
ISBN-13: 978 0 255 36596 3; £10.00

Capitalism – A Condensed Version
Arthur Seldon
Occasional Paper 140
ISBN-13: 978 0 255 36598 7; £7.50

Catholic Social Teaching and the Market Economy
Philip Booth
Hobart Paperback 34
ISBN-13: 978 0 255 36581 9; £15.00

All the listed IEA papers, including those that are out of print, can be downloaded from www.iea.org.uk. Purchases can also be made through the website. To order copies of currently available IEA papers, or to enquire about availability, please contact:

Gazelle
IEA orders
FREEPOST RLYS-EAHU-YSCZ
White Cross Mills
Hightown
Lancaster LA1 4XS

Tel: 01524 68765
Fax: 01524 63232
Email: sales@gazellebooks.co.uk

The IEA also offers a subscription service to its publications. For a single annual payment, currently £40.00 in the UK, you will receive every monograph the IEA publishes during the course of a year and discounts on our extensive back catalogue. For more information, please contact:

Adam Myers
Subscriptions
The Institute of Economic Affairs
2 Lord North Street
London SW1P 3LB

Tel: 020 7799 8920
Fax: 020 7799 2137
Website: www.iea.org.uk